Rancière and Emancipatory Art Pedagogies

Radical Politics and Education

Series editors: Derek R. Ford and Tyson E. Lewis

With movements against oppression and exploitation heightening across the globe, radical activists and researchers are increasingly turning to educational theory to understand the pedagogical aspects of struggle. The Radical Politics and Education series opens a space at this critical juncture, one that pushes past standard expositions of critical education and critical pedagogy. Recognizing the need to push political and educational formulations into new theoretical and practical terrains, the series is an opportunity for activists, political thinkers, and educational philosophers to cross disciplinary divides and meet in common. This kind of dialogue is crucially needed as political struggles are increasingly concerned with questions of how to educate themselves and others, and as educational philosophy attempts to redefine itself beyond academic norms and disciplinary values. This series serves to facilitate new conversations at and beyond these borders.

Advisory Board:

Also available in the series:

Against Sex Education: Pedagogy, Sex Work, and State Violence, Caitlin Howlett

A History of Education for the Many: From Colonization and Slavery to the Decline of US Imperialism, Curry Malott

Experiments in Decolonizing the University: Towards an Ecology of Study, Hans Schildermans

Rethinking Philosophy for Children: Agamben and Education as Pure Means, Tyson E. Lewis and Igor Jasinski

Althusser and Education: Reassessing Critical Education, David I. Backer

A Voice for Maria Favela: An Adventure in Creative Literacy, Antonio Leal

Forthcoming in the series:

Queers Teach This!: Queer and Trans Pleasures, Politics, and Pedagogues, Adam J. Greteman

Rancière and Emancipatory Art Pedagogies

The Politics of Childhood Art

Hayon Park

BLOOMSBURY ACADEMIC
LONDON • NEW YORK • OXFORD • NEW DELHI • SYDNEY

BLOOMSBURY ACADEMIC
Bloomsbury Publishing Plc
50 Bedford Square, London, WC1B 3DP, UK
1385 Broadway, New York, NY 10018, USA
29 Earlsfort Terrace, Dublin 2, Ireland

BLOOMSBURY, BLOOMSBURY ACADEMIC and the Diana logo are trademarks of
Bloomsbury Publishing Plc

First published in Great Britain 2023
This paperback edition published 2024

Series design by Adriana Brioso
Cover image © bortonia/iStock

A catalogue record for this book is available from the British Library.

A catalog record for this book is available from the Library of Congress.

ISBN: HB: 978-1-3502-6918-7
         PB: 978-1-3502-6922-4
       ePDF: 978-1-3502-6919-4
      eBook: 978-1-3502-6920-0

Series: Radical Politics and Education

Typeset by Integra Software Services Pvt. Ltd.

To find out more about our authors and books visit www.bloomsbury.com
and sign up for our newsletters.

Contents

Figures

Acknowledgements

This book is a culmination of my doctoral research on childhood art. I would like to thank first and foremost the kindergarten children and teachers at Bennett Family Center for their participation in this study during the 2017–18 academic year. Thank you for allowing me to observe and be inspired by the wondrous work you do.

On the day of my dissertation defense, Dr. Charles Garoian said, looking at me with his piercing eyes, "You should write this into a book," even before the idea that I had just become a doctor sunk in. I would have never even imagined to write a book if it hadn't come from him, whom I deeply respect for his expertise in art pedagogy and critical thinking, and, importantly, who does not make such suggestions lightly. I am so grateful for his encouragement and guidance. Yet this would not have been materialized if it wasn't Dr. Tyson Lewis's offer to write a proposal for the *Radical Politics and Education* series that he and Dr. Derek Ford co-edit. Thank you.

I have to note here that this book could not have been written without the significant scholarship and care from my former advisor and dearest colleague Dr. Christopher Schulte, who has supported my research from the beginning and has given generous feedback on my writings and other related publications, and Dr. Christine Thompson, who has always given her invaluable time, keen insights, and the necessary courage to preserve.

I want to thank the anonymous peer reviewers of this book for their constructive and helpful suggestions, my editor Molly for thinking with me along this journey, whose clear-eyed vision shaped this book, and Bloomsbury Academic for their support. My gratitude also goes to the School of Art at George Mason University for supporting faculty research and creative endeavors.

Finally, I would like to take this opportunity to thank my family—Mom, Dad, and Julian—for bringing me up with deep trust and security from afar.

Introduction

Carefully curated by the instructors for a still life to be rendered as a charcoal drawing, sixteen metal easels are circled around a table with an assortment of objects neatly placed on a white cloth. The walls that surround us are covered with pictures in three groups: pencil drawings, charcoal still life drawings, and watercolor paintings. It is the beginning of our second four-hour slot of drawing, just after our thirty-minute lunch break. As we begin to draw the still life, we almost always recognize what we are supposed to place as the main object—an item to be sketched bigger than the others, slightly moved off from the center of the paper—and what we could draw as other supporting objects, all composed on a 40 x 60 cm charcoal paper clipped on our easels' wooden panels.

On this day, the main object was a whole green cabbage with the cut end of the stem facing up, with supporting objects placed around it, including a plastic Coca-Cola bottle, an apple, and smaller objects in the background.

From afar, we heard high heels click-clacking down the granite hallway in approach to our studio door. An immediate silence commenced. Ms. Lee walked in and we greeted her with silence—no one said hi to her as we concentrated on the drawing, or at least pretended to. She began to roam the studio with her heels clacking the floor, hands placed on her back, lecturing on the importance of sketching while we all listened in silence. We moved our pencils busily. Meeting a certain time limit to finish our sketch was crucial, normally in the first thirty to forty minutes. In fact, the most frequently used vocabulary in the studio, not only by Ms. Lee but also the other instructors, was "quickly," to prepare us for the time frame at the actual exam.

Ms. Lee emphasized that the oval shape of the cabbage stem had to be more of a round circle, rather than a thin oval, to suggest a wider viewpoint. She instructed us to compare looking at the still life objects from above—where more objects could be captured in a frame, thus allowing more expressions of volume such as light and shade—and from the side—in which only a few objects could fit into the frame as flat volumes. Circling around our easels, she repeated this several times, pointing out who was doing it right.

As I erased the circle-shaped pencil mark to elaborate an even more full circle, Ms. Lee identified my cabbage stem section as having a thin oval shape. She called me out to stand up, walk over to the movable drawer that was often used as a still life placing table, and grab the edges. In a daze, my body moved as ordered before even realizing that this was going to be my first physical punishment from Ms. Lee. She then smacked me with the plastic ruler three times. Thwack! Thwack! Thwack! Then, my body began to move again, quietly retreating to my seat to resume drawing. I reminded myself to immediately correct that "damn flat oval." I corrected the cabbage top (which I was about to re-sketch just moments before Ms. Lee's decision to punish me), then proceeded to render the supporting objects.

A Disciplinary Police

Children being punished in an art studio may not be commonly encountered today, especially in an American context. However, it was the opposite during my childhood in Seoul, South Korea in the early 2000s, at least at the studio I attended. During the time of the year when the preparation for the prestigious arts middle school entrance exam became rigorous, the art hagwons offered intensive art lessons for sixth graders to prepare for the exam.[1] Translated as "educational institute" in Korean, hagwon (학원) is a private institute typically available within walking distance of the neighborhood, where registered students take art lessons in small studio environments, paying monthly tuitions. A hagwon could specify in any area for any ages: there are hagwons of school subject areas (e.g., math and English) and hagwons that are non-school-subject oriented, which specialize in subjects such as learning ballet or cooking. In terms of art hagwons, there are traditionally two types: the art hagwons for preK to sixth grade students function primarily as after-school childcare spaces, focusing more on exploring diverse art materials and techniques; and the art hagwons for middle and high school students who plan to major in art or design in secondary school or college emphasize the development of fundamental and advanced art and design skills. In the latter type of hagwons, forms, representation, color theories, and the mastery of traditional materials and skills are emphasized to help registered students prepare for specialized art schools' entrance examinations (see also Shin & Kim, 2014).

The annual art-specialized middle school entrance exam, typically held in late October, consisted of creating two types of artworks in one day. The first 3.5 hours was dedicated to an imaginary watercolor painting. Then, after a lunch break, a second 3.5-hour period focused on the creation of a still life charcoal drawing. In preparation for taking the exam, the art hagwon I attended, among many other art hagwons in South Korea, required that students spend a total of 13 hours per day at the art hagwon from the beginning of summer break (around mid-July) to the exam day, and three four-hour classes and two thirty-minute meal breaks in between, which meant that students skipped school for the first half of fall semester.

During a four-hour class time, there would be two instructors present if it were a regular class, and one instructor if it was a mock exam. In regular classes, though for the majority of the time we worked on our own paintings or drawings, the instructor might take the time to sit down on a student's chair and directly add, correct, and develop the work. Because the personal touch of the adult helped students to learn how to enhance the level of the drawing, the instructor(s) did this for all students two to three times a class. The mock exam, however, was based solely on the work of the students. Within the context of a mock exam, the role of the instructor was to therefore supervise and remind students of the time that remained. As such, our works done as an exam were usually evaluated and ranked, with the occasional letter grade being added to the upper right side of a finished work.

Fortunately, because my works were frequently ranked among the best, or perhaps because my mother was an acquaintance of Ms. Lee, the head instructor of the art hagwon, I ostensibly evaded such embarrassing moments, yet was always tormented with the recurring atmosphere of punishment and fear. Ms. Lee was the authoritative figure who instructed verbally more than holding the pencil or brush. She was in her early forties at that time and had a near mythic aura; perfectly applied makeup with mid-length salon curls, and, most interestingly, an all-black attire that always included a black flare maxi dress dropped down to her ankles. There was even a rumor circulating at the time, that once and only once had Ms. Lee been spotted wearing blue jeans. As the story goes, she was shopping at a neighborhood grocery store. This, coupled with her infrequent visits, which centered mostly on making announcements and having everyone gather around one student's work to highlight the "right" way to draw, only added to her mystique.

Ms. Lee's presence and instruction urged us to draw/paint faster, rank and evaluate each other after a mock exam, and even to evaluate and judge the quality of our maintenance work (e.g., asking us to clean up our eating area, checking our watercolor palettes for abundant amount of paint prepared, resolving peer issues, etc.) of the duration of her appearance could be from a few seconds to up to an hour—she never stayed the full four-hour class time since there were other groups to supervise such as secondary school students preparing for the arts high school or college.

It was not only her appearance that was witch-like but also her performances. As the exam approached, her instructional methods became more rigorous and authoritarian. She often scolded students by yelling or spanking them with a clear 50 cm plastic ruler for various reasons, mostly when the technical rules of drawing or painting were not followed. Those who were yelled at or spanked were frequently the ones who we tacitly thought of as less talented, not competent enough to get into the art schools. At times, it was often the two boys among the sixteen sixth graders who the girls felt less sorry for, for being punished. However, the day we drew the cabbage was different. Somehow, this day, Ms. Lee was present in the classroom from the beginning, from our initial stage of sketching still life objects with pencils to the later stage of drawing with charcoal.

This discipline-and-punishment-based art education lives with me as an inscribed mark on my personal history of art education. There were clear lines that could not be crossed: "correct" skills to sketch still life figures, "proper" time spent to complete a work of drawing, and "expected" ways of receiving punishment from the art instructor. It was a haunting experience, if not traumatic, to all of the students.

I recall one of the girls disclosing to me on the exam day that she had been taking sleeping aids every night because Ms. Lee would visit her in her dreams. Ms. Lee—or rather the ghost of Ms. Lee—was perhaps haunting us more so in her absence, as we feared for her unforeseeable visits, unpredictable mood, and the unfathomable ways she punished and shamed us. It was the possibility of return, her coming and going, that scared us waking or sleeping. The scene of punishment conjured up in our minds the moment we heard the clacking of footsteps, along with the fear of not knowing what to expect were always present. There was no closure to this recurring fear; even when the teachers were not present, we *found* the imagery and voices in the midst of their vacancy. Though the end of the exam might have liberated us from any physical punishment, it has lived with me throughout childhood and young adulthood.

Not all of my childhood art education involved haunting experiences. I was an avid artist who would draw anytime and anywhere. At home, my mother, who studied fine arts in college, always encouraged me to draw and paint, providing me with a variety of art materials to consider and explore, even her "quality" art materials.

My mother often drew with me using her great sense and realistic techniques of figure drawing, which made me wish to draw as well as her. Even earlier, at the Montessori daycare center I went to in Champaign, Illinois, I drew freely whenever I could, as the teachers encouraged my creative endeavors, along with other material choices that I made as a child. Despite my art education experience as an older child and teenager in Korea, it was my time at home— drawing with my mother—and my early experiences of that choice-based, child-centered early childhood education that left an imprint on my life as an artist and art learner.

Considering my rigorous personal history of art learning and practices, it comes as no surprise that I was utterly fascinated by the artistic engagements of children at my first research experience, somewhat romanticizing children's art practices to a certain extent. Initially, I explored children's art as a form of play (Park, 2018), then also broadened my perspective to the social aspects and peer relationships that surround the art experiences. Being around young children to observe, listen to, and engage with their art making was an experience that was dramatically different from those I had while attending the art hagwon in Korea. However, as I moved further into my endeavor of doing ethnographic fieldwork for researching childhood art and became more involved in the everyday lives of the children, I realized that childhood art is not merely about being playful, cute, imaginary, or developmentally conducive, but rather consists of intricately woven, complex matters and events that involve subtle to explicit political acts. That is to say, in observing the process of children's art practice, which was often accompanied by verbal narratives, I began to notice more clearly the politics that inform and surround children's art making. There were solitary declarations, such as: "I am an artist and I can do/paint/draw whatever I want." There were questions of solidarity among peers: "We're artists, right?" And there were disclosures of concern, too: "Are we allowed to do that?" or "I don't think [the teacher] will be happy about this."

Along with the actions associated with such narratives, I view these doings as inherently political, as gestures that reveal children's continuous negotiation of the adults' rules and the children's own desire to make themselves seen and heard, to legitimatize their ontological status and their experiences in the classroom. In other words, the politics revealed the in-between status in which children are situated, a status in which it is necessary to both reside and also move between the adults' world and their own, constantly having to negotiate the ideas and interests of adults, and at times their mere presence. In focusing on the politics visible in childhood art, this book attempts to argue for a reconsideration of early childhood art and its pedagogies so that emancipatory ways of thinking become possible.

Childhood Art and Emancipatory Pedagogies

At the art hagwon in Korea, we were nothing more than docile beings. The unspoken assumption was that we lacked the ability to produce appropriate artworks qualifying for the exams, and therefore our art skills would improve if we were given the proper training and education. Surely, the most apparent problem of this art education derives from South Korea's art school exam system where the middle school's enrollment requires rigorous training beyond what was taught in elementary school art classes, along with the heated extracurricular education culture influenced by "helicopter moms" (Park et al., 2015) or "tiger parenting" (Juang et al., 2013). However, it is one example of childhood images that rooted from a long history of Western theories that perpetuated the distributed sensible toward children's lives. That is, as not-yet artists, not-yet autonomous beings competent to learn art by ourselves, our bodies were treated and seen in particular ways, malleable to the adults' power. This assumption on us as a less-than being was vividly present in every social engagement at the art hagwon, generating fears to the individual, as well as the peer culture as a group. This personal experience is what inspired the study of childhood art in the United States during my graduate studies. I wished to engage deeply in young children's art to an extent that would allow me to find subtle yet undeniable struggles within childhood art. In other words, my question is: what kind of politics might be present in and about childhood art?

To address this, in this book I turn to the thoughts of French philosopher Jacques Rancière (1940–) to inquire what political actions children might manifest as the "aesthetic in principle" (Rancière, 1999, p. 58) through art, especially in classroom settings. For example, Rancière's notion of "the distribution of the sensible"—a society's decision-making process, specifically the problem of who gets to be visible and invisible, sayable and unsayable, audible and inaudible, legible and illegible—creates an aesthetic *partitioning* of the realm of the perceivable in society, which positions certain bodies as subjects while other bodies are seen as mere objects. As a result, the composition of a community gets to be defined by certain sensory distribution. However, Rancière views that when those who are seen as objects disagree with their given partitions, a political enactment emerges. As a relational matter in nature, the essence of politics resides in "dissensus" (Rancière, 2015) which entails an interruption of the "distribution of the sensible," where political subjects— namely, those who are considered less than equal in a given distribution of the sensible—make themselves visible and legible beings. I view this act of dissensus as being integral to children's everyday lives, because children are social beings who live in social environments, constantly having to negotiate between the adults' world and their own world (Corsaro, 2015).

Though one of Rancière's most recognized works, *The Ignorant Schoolmaster: Five Lessons in Intellectual Emancipation* (1991) established a foundation on pedagogy, some scholars find that Rancière's work provided significantly less understanding of the politics and aesthetics of education, compared to that offered in his concentration on the aesthetics of politics and the aesthetic regime of art as political (Lewis, 2012). Aligning with this idea, I try to find ways in which my study could fill in the gaps of what Rancière might have overlooked in the realm of education and the arts.

To do this, it is important to identify what kind of policing forces exist in the conventional theories and practices of early childhood art education. This is not to say that Rancière's ideas are foreign to the field of art education. In fact, Rancièrian thoughts have been adapted to generate productive discussions for the field, for example, on its relation to urban youth (Trafí-Prats, 2012), artists with disabilities (Richardson (Eisenhauer), 2018), and contemporary art practices (Lewis, 2015; Pérez Miles, 2016; Richardson & Richardson (Eisenhauer), 2020; Thumlert, 2015). Yet there have been few studies that draw on Rancière's ideas in relation to early childhood art practices, and this book aims to fill that empty space.

Children, in many ways, are always having to "leave the interpretation of their own lives to another age group," that is, adults, "whose interests are potentially at odds with those of themselves" (Qvortrup et al., 1994, p. 6). Considering how young children are a structurally marginalized population illustrated as social objects often associated with *less than* narratives—as dependent, deficient, passive, and in need of adult intervention—I find Rancière's interpretation of politics reserved for "part of those who have no part [*la part des sans-part*]" (Rancière, 1999, p. 11) particularly compelling. Much of what we have come to "know" and seem to "value" about childhood art has emerged from a logic and approach that often regards the child and children's knowledge, work, and experience as being less than our own. In the field of art education, this logic and its attendant approach are most aptly identified in terms of research and theory that, especially during the mid-twentieth century, focused foremost on the causality between children's art and issues of their intellectual, emotional, and cognitive development (e.g., Arnheim, 1974; Gardner, 1980; Kellogg, 1969). The goal was to recognize children's social and cultural agency, and adult expectations of particular "child-like" styles and the "myth of inherent creativity" (McClure, 2011, p. 127) seem to persist in everyday curriculum and pedagogy. As a result of this focus, existing knowledge in the field continues to be dominated by developmental psychology (Burman, 2017) and accounts of children's drawings based on such perspectives (e.g., Lowenfeld & Brittain, 1947). These understandings of children's thinking, making, and living are predetermined, limit children's voice and agency, routinely decontextualize the child and their work, and ultimately position children to be the subject of adult intervention. Although these theories of classification were developed with the best of intentions, fashioned for a better understanding of young people's art, such accounts have nonetheless functioned in service to discourses that are inclined to regard children as deficient or defiant, as Other, especially when children's work fails to echo certain normalized characteristics and models.

As there are many other elements adults fail to notice, the event of children's art always exceeds the idea that it is a "thing" which can be arranged into developmental stages, a practice that can always be tamed and organized, and made to be predictable. In other words, the art making of children is such that it often exists between stages, is suitable to multiple stages at once, or evades them entirely, "making a mockery of neat categorization" (Duncum, 2018, p. 225).

Along with Rancièrian thinking, throughout the book I consistently engage with post-structural and reconceptualistic theorizations of childhood studies. If the socially and historically constructed accounts of children's lives and their works have been prone to compartmentalizing the child, children, and children's art making, reconceptualistic approaches posit a critical stance toward such understandings so that we understand the contextualized, multiple cultural experiences of childhood.

Within the reconceptualistic study of childhood and children's works, I also subscribe to postdevelopmental approaches of childhood art. As Sakr and Osgood (2019) note, "postdevelopmental" neither indicates anti-developmental nor suggests a neat break between developmental and postdevelopmental thinking. It is rather to explore alternative ways of seeing children's art while recognizing the importance of developmentalist conceptualizations. Additionally, some statements may align with post-humanistic and new materialistic ideas, for example I elaborate on the material affects in children's art practice in Chapter 4. Yet I approach this with caution. As much as I believe in and wish to highlight nonhuman affects (e.g., objects, space, digital media) in childhood art, I am aware of the fact that children, in many ways, have not been considered "humans" in the first place compared to heteronormative adults (e.g., Kromidas, 2014). As such, to decenter the humans that had not attained a premise of humanity into a flattened ontology, especially in the realm of childhood art research, seems antithetical to my purpose of research and the writing of this book. As Peter Kraftl (2020) writes, the decentering is "not enough" and "too much" (p. 5). Rather, I try to propose a perspective that attends to the particularities of childhood and children's artistic practices, how a focus on the politics might contribute to seeing the multiple, contextualized understandings of childhood art.

Though a move toward multiple perspectives on children's art has been made in recent decades (e.g., Duncum, 2018; Ivashkevich, 2009; Kukkonen & Chang-Kredl, 2018; McClure, 2011; Pearson, 2001; Sakr & Osgood, 2019; Schulte, 2011, 2015a, 2015b, 2021; Schulte & Thompson, 2018; Thompson, 2009; Wilson & Wilson, 1981), it has often been associated with a specific style, particularly those which are made in the school setting. Art education scholar Arthur Efland (1976) wrote that the "school art style" prevails in the art classrooms, which is a style that Wilson (2004) noted as "the appearance of creativity" (p. 277). In this sense, I use "childhood art" with an intention to signify a broader sense of art that emerges in childhood, that also is grounded on the underpinnings of childhood studies and childhood art education. It is also an attempt to embrace the various modes of practices, pedagogies, and learning associated with the art in childhood. I also occasionally use the term "children's art" when referring to my research participants' artistic engagements. Importantly, though, in the rare cases I use "child art," it often refers to a specific collection of narratives that have long been written by a variety of groups—psychologists, anthropologists, art historians, policy makers, educators, and artists—since the late nineteenth century. Art education scholar Brent Wilson (1974) identified the characteristics of child art as something that has

> seldom been allowed into our highly controlled art classes. It is the spontaneous play art of young people. ... It has little of the polished lushness of art classroom art, but once one learns to look at tatty little drawings done in ball point on lined paper, a whole world of excitement unfolds. From play art we can learn why young people make art in the first place and why some keep on making it while others stop.
>
> (p. 3, as cited in Efland, 1976)

The childhood art that resides between the traditional, rule-governed, teacher-led art practices and the art made by children's desire is what I am interested in. I find this type of childhood art situated in the liminal space where distinct practices of art conflicts, discussions, and negotiations take place and, therefore creating a potential foundation for politics to emerge of young children's art might provoke new and different understandings for childhood art.

Leaning onto Rancière's idea of emancipation, I consider what emancipatory art pedagogies might look like in childhood art. Emancipatory pedagogies have been taken up by many past and contemporary thinkers, especially following Paulo Freire's defense of emancipatory education. While Freire's *Pedagogy of the Oppressed* (2000) presented an unprecedented force, it became tamed throughout the late twentieth century until Marxist and neo-Marxist educators who wished to imagine a new language for educational critique and knowledge-producing augmented it. However, today, little has changed. Capitalistic logic hinders the emergence of new thoughts, let alone educational transformation, thus perpetuating existing beliefs and systems that are often a disservice to education.

Although Rancière is traditionally not identified as part of the school of critical pedagogy, his thoughts on education, as seen in *The Ignorant Schoolmaster: Five Lessons in Intellectual Emancipation* (1991), are highly predicated on the idea of emancipation. A Rancièrian thinking of emancipation is more about verifying existing political subjectivities (of students) that makes possible a redistribution of the sensible, moving against any given partitions and placements. In fact, for both Freire and Rancière, educational practices are far from neutral, as they determine to a great extent on the fate of our placements in the society (see Lewis, 2012; Vlieghe, 2018). Moreover, when referring to pedagogy or the pedagogical work, I think of theories of learning, practices of teaching, bodies of knowledge and skills, methodologies, and modes of assessment, along with many other relational matters that concern the immanence of a particular child's mode of learning and creative practices.

What I mean by *emancipatory art pedagogies*, therefore, is not so much about pedagogies as a vehicle for emancipation, but rather pedagogies of art that steer us away from normalized sensibles and enable us to attend to the politics of art and education—ways to think and do differently. Simply put, Rancière's notion of emancipation is using one's intelligence based on the assumption of the equality of intelligence. The use of the plural (pedagogies) is also intentional. I want to emphasize that my stance in thinking about emancipatory pedagogies is not to discover the one right answer but to imagine multiple approaches toward emancipatory pedagogical practices. This is not to suggest, though, that visual art pedagogy has not been diverse. Art pedagogy, the practice of teaching in the art, promotes multiple understandings by nature, as art cannot be taught by a one-right method. In fact, the field of art education has been grounded on multiple nationwide and international movements concerned with the theories and practices of art, such as Discipline-Based Art Education (Eisner, 1988), Visual Culture Art Education (Freedman, 2003; Tavin & Hausman, 2004; Wilson, 2003), Multicultural Art Education (Chalmers, 1996), and a/r/tography (Irwin & de Cosson, 2004). These movements most certainly contributed to the expansion of the field of art education in classrooms as well as research, creating opportunities for the research and pedagogical practices to be valued. This recognition—that children's relations to art practice and pedagogy are situated and shifting—not only changes how we think about and approach children's experiences of making and learning in the visual arts but is also a recognition that materializes in dramatically different ways across cultures, communities, and contexts. For this reason, I believe it is essential that questions be formulated that are critical in orientation to the widening scope of factors that contribute to decisions about what ideas and processes get to matter in childhood art, as these shape the contours in which art practices and pedagogies are understood, valued, and practiced. In viewing the subtle and often unnoticed inequality surrounding childhood art as an urgent matter, I explore emancipatory art pedagogies by thinking experimentally with Rancière.

What I am proposing by exploring childhood art through Rancièrian thoughts then is to offer an alternative perspective to the assumptions that underwrite disciplinary knowledge, that of constructing a canon of central ideas and texts that make up a field. Working against linear, structural models that tidy up what is replete with uncertainties (i.e., developmental psychology), imagining emancipatory pedagogies is to think proliferation and contamination over the field's attempts to fully represent knowledge about children and childhood. It is also my contention that along with our endeavors to understand the unknown we must also work against our very efforts to know. In other words, we as adults interested in or working with children carry the ethical obligation to question conventional modes of knowing.

Chapter Outlines

Rancière and Emancipatory Art Pedagogies: The Politics of Childhood Art is theoretical in orientation, supported by ethnographic examples. I attempt to balance the theoretical exploration of children's art through the academic literature on childhood studies, children's art, and the philosophical writings of Jacques Rancière, as well as provide ample examples from my experience of engaging with children and their artistic practices. Attuned to Rancière's (1989) idea of writing, I write this book with particular attention to how my practice of writing about children might also be nonhierarchical and produce a sense of equality. I endeavor to weave the political philosophy in each chapter and highlight its relation to childhood art. I do so by bringing my research at a university-affiliated kindergarten classroom in the United States to reflect on the experiences through a methodology that I am calling *aesthetico-ethnography*. As part of the ethnographic characteristics, my simultaneous position as an artist, educator, researcher, and the writer of this book plays a crucial role.

Chapter 1, "Thinking Pedagogy, Politics, and Aesthetics with Jacques Rancière," serves as a brief review of Rancière's elaboration on three main concepts: pedagogy, politics, and aesthetics. First, in the discussion of pedagogy, I primarily refer to *The Ignorant Schoolmaster* (1991) followed by an illustration of Rancière's relationship with his mentor, Louis Althusser, which embodied the concept of "ignorance" and emancipation from the master. In presenting Rancière's account of democratic politics, I build up on the previous discussion of pedagogical "dissensus" as seen in *The Ignorant Schoolmaster* in order to provoke the idea that politics is immanent in everyday life. Specifically, I attend to Oliver Davis's (2010) emphasis on four main points of Rancièrian politics as a framework. This clarifies a somewhat broad account of politics: (1) politics as an opposition to "police"; (2) Rancière's structural account of democratic politics; (3) the theory of political "subjects" and "subjectivation";

and (4) the aesthetic dimensions to politics (pp. 74–100). The third focus, aesthetics, is also inseparable from the preceding discussion of "politics" as a persuasion of equality, inasmuch as Rancière views politics and aesthetics as synonymous in terms of its egalitarian suspension of the hierarchical modes of representation. Here, I describe Rancière's conceptualization of the three regimes in which art has been primarily situated—the *ethical, representational,* and the *aesthetic*—followed by a discussion on how dissensual politics and aesthetics could be seen in childhood studies and children's art.

Chapter 2 examines the discourse of childhood studies and its relation to art education theories and practices by drawing on Derrida's (1994) conception of "hauntology." I illustrate a historical landscape of (1) the images of childhood, and (2) childhood art that have bound children into partitions based on age-based developmental criteria, which I attempt to challenge via Rancièrian concepts. First, I adopt James, Jenks, and Prout's (1998) review of the theoretical models of childhood, from the "pre-sociological" characterization (i.e., the innocent child, the naturally developing child, etc.), to "sociological," to grasp the conventional perceptions of child(ren) and childhood. In addition, I dedicate a section for thinking about the citizenship of children, as it attributes to children's reality of being "part of those that have no part" (Rancière, 2015, p. 33) of the distribution of the sensible. Then, I turn to the discussion of the study of childhood art that has also been bound to specific knowledge systems and thus subjugated to the generalizable as part of the distribution of the sensible. I focus on two main aspects of art education literature: aesthetics and contents.

In Chapter 3, I elaborate on the methodological approach of this study by discussing ethnography in childhood studies and how the distribution of the sensible might exist in ethnographic practices. In doing so, I inquire as to how the aesthetic dimension, in Rancièrian terms, might emerge in ethnographic practices and call my approach as an aesthetico-ethnographic case study. I discuss how the methodological approach of the study of childhood art has been established upon a Rancièrian lens, specifically how the concept of "aesthetics" demands the researcher disrupt her preconceived notions about the subject and thus constitute effects of equality with the participants. As this study is based on an ethnographic case study of kindergarteners' art practices, I briefly unpack how the method is neither solely "ethnographic" nor "case study" but an approach that attempts to embody aesthetics by practicing a supposition of equality between the often-hierarchical dynamics of researcher/participants, adult/child, teacher/students, etc. I bring in my observation of how children also manifest their capability to disagree with and overturn the existing rules and roles imposed on them by constituting a political scene, despite the struggle that might follow.

The fourth chapter focuses on a painting event I encountered at the kindergarten classroom, in which two boys diverged from the teacher's instruction of painting small dots yet continued to be cognizant of the teacher's presence and rules. I consider this as a political enactment drawing upon Rancière's notion of politics and aesthetics. Specifically, in examining the painting event, I focus on the *politics* children attended to, whereby a sense of tension and thrill was demonstrated as a community, as well as the *aesthetic* experience that was being produced in conjunction with the political enactments, along with other related concepts."

The fifth chapter explores Rancière's concept of "ignorance" in relation to my experience of drawing popular culture figures with children in the kindergarten classroom, where I developed a role of an "artist in residence" who would draw for and with children, upon their request. Specifically, this chapter attends to a drawing event, in which a five-year-old boy, Alex, initially asked me to draw Star Wars characters for him, then worked collaboratively with me in order to complete the drawing as he desired. Primarily drawing on the ideas of Ranciére, along with brief discussion on "response-ability" (Haraway, 2016), I suggest that a kind of intellectual equality can be produced through the deliberate presupposition of ignorance and the activation of a will to un-know, which thereby enables the child and adult to attend with greater care to the negotiation of knowledge and culture in the context of drawing. Through this suggestion, I contend that educators, or interested adults, more broadly, practice a relational ethics of ignorance.

By way of a conclusion, the last part of this book addresses to the "so what?" question that might arise for readers. First, based on my observation that, among the diverse topics and artistic modes Rancière writes about, childhood art and its pedagogy is out of the picture, I discuss the implications of Rancière leaving out children's art in the discussion of the aesthetic regime of art. Then, I explore how Tyson Lewis's (2016b) concept of "curiosity" might offer the ways in which to attend to a better police order, thus emancipation, and how it could be at the center of our practices that moves toward emancipatory art pedagogies.

My study of the politics of childhood art is committed to expanding the understanding of childhood art by focusing on children's art practices that escape the normalized accounts, and which are therefore seen as political. Rather than a mere application of Rancière's thoughts to the study of early childhood art and education, the major goal of this work is to explore the different sensibilities in the discourse of childhood art that are required when understanding and responding to children's politico-aesthetic manifestations. As the field of knowledge and practice in art education grows, how might recognizing the politics of childhood art take an important role in diversifying perspectives? I make the claim that recognizing the politics of childhood art is a necessary foray into the diversity of regimes of thought that exist in early childhood education and art education—it is an effort toward emancipatory pedagogy that paradoxically originates from not knowing as a way of knowing.

Thinking Pedagogy, Politics, and Aesthetics with Jacques Rancière

The work of Jacques Rancière has been increasingly influential in the field of visual arts and art education for its radical view of education, arts, politics, and aesthetics, though these concepts are quite distinct from the everyday use of such words. His ideas have their foundation on his personal experience as one who studied as a mentee of Louis Althusser in late twentieth century, particularly around the time of May 1968 student uprising in Paris.

Rancière unapologetically looks for ways to overturn socially constructed forms of classification or distinction, that is, to destabilize norms of representation that might allow for differentiating one class of person or experience from another. For example, a common thread that permeates his work is to subvert the less-than class or groups of people (e.g., workers, students, the inarticulate, viewers, etc.) being policed by the normalized power-holding class (e.g., intellectuals, masters, the articulate, artists, etc.). In seeing that his ideas provide insight for understanding another socially oppressed group (i.e., children), I present this first chapter focusing on Rancière's distribution of the sensible, as well as his ideas about police, ignorance, politics, equality, and aesthetics to see how they resonate with my study of childhood art.

The Distribution of the Sensible

Jacques Rancière argues that societies are structured according to *le partage du sensible*, translated as the "partition of the perceptible" or the "distribution of the sensible."

> I call the distribution of the sensible the system of self-evident facts of sense perception that simultaneously discloses the existence of something in common and the determinations that define the respective parts and positions within it. The distribution of the sensible reveals who can have a share in what is common to the community based on what they do and on the time and space in which this activity is performed … it defines what is visible or not in a common space, endowed with a common language, etc. There is thus an "aesthetics" at the core of politics … It is a delimitation of spaces and times, of the visible and the invisible of speech and noise, that simultaneously determines the place and the stakes of politics as a form of experience. Politics revolves around what is seen and what can be said about it, around who has the ability to see and the talent to speak, around the properties of spaces and the possibilities of time.
>
> (Rancière, 2013a, pp. 12–13)

The distribution of sensible is composed of the *a priori* laws that condition what is possible to see and hear, to say and think, to do and make. It is the condition of what is possible to apprehend by the senses, such as the possibility for perception, thought, and activity, rather than something that makes sense. The sensible is partitioned into various regimes that delimits forms of inclusion and exclusion in a community. To put the distribution of the sensible into everyday language, it is the existing frameworks of knowledge that define people's modalities of visibility, audibility, and performativity by an aesthetic organization, which regard certain bodies as subjects while others are seen as objects—in other words, it is "a matter of constructing a plot" (Rancière, 2016, p. 29).

Then, who holds the power to construct the plot? Who decides meaning of the plot and what gets to be mere subjects in the plot? Rancière's elaboration on the power of the *police* helps us answer these questions.

> The police is thus first an order of bodies that defines the allocation of ways of doing, ways of being, and ways of saying, and sees that those bodies are assigned by name to a particular place and task; it is a particular order of the visible and the sayable that sees that a particular activity is visible and another is not, that this speech is discourse and another is noise.
>
> (Rancière, 1999, p. 29)

It is notable that there are *order(s)* of the police, the qualitatively different and more or less desirable arrangement the police renders. The existence of an order implies that an established consensus or a force decides to prioritize, sort, group, align, or eliminate particular qualities or bodies out of the mix. Thus, we inhabit an order of the police at any given time, and by definition it obscures and renders unrecognizable portions of the population. The group constituting the police, in this sense, is a particular distributed sensible that defines the territory one should occupy and the accordingly expected activity of the allocated position.

Going back to the focus of this study, it is important to note that the presence of police materializes in various forms at schools: the instructional methods, curricula, classroom rules, and even the environment of the classrooms, to name a few. As the power of police defines the ways of doing and being, bodies in educational institutions are also expected to operate by police order. In thinking specifically about art education, a school art curriculum might be constructed as a plot that decides, for example, what types of art could be seen as approvable art while others are not, or what narratives could be told through art while others cannot. This message could be insinuated in subtle forms, such as the "good" examples hung on classroom walls, the given materials and rules about particular ways of using them, and/or the teacher's lesson plans. Accordingly, by these policed senses, the students' bodies become assigned to a particular place and task; it is a particular distribution of the sensible constructed to dictate a particular aesthetics and performance acceptable in the space.

This idea of the distribution of the sensible by police power not only resonates with my personal experience at the hagwon, but also evokes encounters at the kindergarten classroom during my ethnographic fieldwork. In examining children's art practices at the classroom, I have come to realize that there is, too, a policing in the discipline even when children are supposedly encouraged to be free in activating their creativity: during early childhood. Though it may be a different degree of policing than what my peers and I experienced at the hagwon, the kindergarteners also desired to gain approval and appreciation from the adults (e.g., parents and teachers), which often accompanied a simultaneous fear of rejection, undervalue, or shame. Although the fear often subsides upon the encouraging responses of adults, an elusive yet perpetual force of the police seems to persist in children's perception of art education.

Another evident reality of the distribution of the sensible (Rancière, 2013a) prevails in children's everyday lives as ghosts: the ghost of developmental partitions, innocent child images, and many other less-than narratives that can be conjured up again anytime. Inasmuch as ghosts allow us to recognize the normalized discourses that continue to haunt children, I respectfully invite the ghosts as a productive tool to provide avenues of new ideas (Dernikos et al., 2019; Gordon, 1997/2008). As an artist, researcher, educator, and a former child learner whose artistic practices were profoundly haunted by adults' implicit and explicit forms of control, I believe it is my moral obligation to address the haunting distribution of the sensible in the scholarship of art education, and more specifically, early childhood art education, insofar as it tends to compartmentalize children into divisive structures. Thus, recognizing such distribution of the sensible prevalent in art education, I am committed to offer potential approaches to actively *think* and *act* against reproducing oppression toward children by aligning myself with the scholars who endeavor to assuage the ghosts, suggesting alternative narratives of children's lives and works. This is why Rancière's ideas are compelling: his thoughts suggest something fundamentally different from the common sense, a sense which enables complicity, and which we perpetuate through our daily routines. In other words, Rancièrian thoughts support my deliberate troubling of this subtle *tendency* that is, the elusive yet prevalent norms that have been accepted but rarely questioned. It is the "ghostly matter" (Gordon, 1997/2008) of the distribution of the sensible that Rancière brings to surface.

The following part explores and examines how Rancière's concept of pedagogy, politics, and aesthetics produce possibilities for alleviating such hauntings, or at least minimize the perpetuation of the distribution of the sensible in understanding the lives and works of children. In other words, how might Rancière's work function as a theoretical framework for this study, and even broader, for producing different understandings that dissociate from the normative images and realities of children? The discussion on intellectual emancipation also serves as a foundation for the following chapters where I further discuss the politics and aesthetics of children's art practice and research methodology.

Pedagogy: The Practice of Ignorance

Among the many ways in which Rancière's philosophical work has been taken up, his elaboration on "intellectual equality" has been the most radical and well-known idea, which also foregrounds his thinking on the concepts of politics and aesthetics. Rancière's conceptualization of intellectual equality is addressed most extensively in *The Ignorant Schoolmaster: Five Lessons in Intellectual Emancipation* (1991), where he provides a distinctive and insightful account of a pedagogical event to argue the importance of affirming equality for an emancipatory epistemology of ignorance. He does this by examining the case of Joseph Jacotot, a French university lecturer in the nineteenth century who proclaimed that all people, including the uneducated, could learn for themselves without a teacher's explanation and that the teacher could, in turn, teach himself what he was ignorant of. This claim originates in Jacotot's unexpected experience of finding himself teaching a class whose members speak exclusively Flemish. Jacotot did not know their language and the students did not know his. He nonetheless organized the lesson around a bilingual edition of the classic French novel *Télémaque,* which was a text Jacotot and the students could not study together. Instead, through an interpreter, Joseph Jacotot asked the students to read half of the book with the aid of translation and the other half quickly, and then write what they had thought about it in French.

The students learned to read *Télémaque* in the same way as learning their mother tongue language: "by observing and retaining, repeating and verifying, by relating what they were trying to know to what they already knew, by doing and reflecting about what they had done" (Rancière, 1991, p. 10). Having expected regrettable outcomes, Jacotot became surprised by the quality of the students' work. As the students looked for the French vocabularies that corresponded with those they already knew, they learned to put the words together to create sentences in French by themselves. As Jacotot describes it, "their spelling and grammar became more and more exact as they progressed through the book; but above all, sentences of writers and not of schoolchildren" (Rancière, 1991, p. 4). Here, what "schoolchildren" might allude to is the conventional and commonly understood role of students who are rarely considered legitimate writers, which suggests the less-than model of children to a certain extent. Nevertheless, as they wrote and learned the language through an unconventional method, it resulted in producing exceptional literary texts. Although Jacotot had explained virtually nothing, neither the spellings nor conjugations of the language, both the students and Jacotot explored the text and found alternative ways to learn through taking the position of un-knowing—the act of *ignorance*.

What is the virtue of ignorance, which Rancière believes is the most important quality of a schoolmaster? To respond to this question, I find it effective to illustrate what the ignorant schoolmaster does and chooses not to do. To begin with, an ignorant schoolmaster is not a teacher who does not teach, but "a teacher who teaches that which is unknown to him or her" (Rancière, 2010, p. 1). The schoolmaster does not teach *his* knowledge but instead commands students to explore what they are able to see, what they think about it, and then to verify it. In practicing ignorance, the schoolmaster intentionally dissociates with his preexisting knowledge about things in order to discover the unknown. By doing so, the only knowledge the ignorant schoolmaster owns becomes the "knowledge of ignorance" (Rancière, 2009a)—the skill to acknowledge his own incapacity. It is a realization that no direct link is necessary between teaching and possessing knowledge.

Characterizing the ignorant schoolmaster, however, is not to say that a teacher is powerless, unknowledgeable, or merely a symbolic status who lacks authority. It is, in fact, the authority of Jacotot that installed the experimental learning experience with students, as he acknowledged his privileged position capable of directing the students according to his experiment. An ignorant schoolmaster retains authority while situating students in a position to actualize intellectual capacities they already possess.

Jacotot refrained from teaching *his* knowledge but instead attempted to move students to explore what they see, what they think about, and to then verify it. Here, intellectual capacity does not mean equal intelligence in terms of numerically measurable IQs, but rather the act of believing that all people are capable of discovering the meaning of diverse things by themselves, just as every child is sufficiently capable of learning a new language. The replication of the process of acquiring their first language (e.g., listening, comparing, repeating, attempting, and imitating) leveraged the students' learning of a new language.

Moreover, an ignorant schoolmaster is ignorant of a particular definition of what he or she is supposed to be as a schoolmaster. Jacotot actively refuses the knowledge of a predetermined identity, which contributed to the rise of the pedagogical experience. Indeed, the pedagogical experience came about as Jacotot refrained from assuming the conventional role of a teacher, which is to say that Jacotot worked against the tendency to give unilateral lectures based on the method of explication. Nor did the students abide by the roles traditionally expected of them, namely, to passively listen to and assume the pre-defined lessons of explication. Explication, according to Rancière, is the "myth of pedagogy, the parable of a world divided into knowing minds and ignorant ones, ripe minds and immature ones, the capable and the incapable, the intelligent and the stupid" (1991, p. 6). To Rancière, explication is an act of stultification. Meaning, when a master explains, he or she transmits standardized knowledge and exercises power to verify if the student has satisfactorily understood what was explained. Rancière (2010) writes:

> The practice of explanation is something completely different from a practical means of reaching some end. It is an end itself, the infinite verification of a fundamental axiom: the axiom of inequality. To explain something to one who is ignorant is, first and foremost, to explain that which would not be understood if it were not explained. It is to demonstrate incapacity.
>
> (p. 3)

As the act of explication only confirms the hierarchical order between the one who explains and the other who to whom explications are given, it indicates that the two reside in distinct partitions. Explication intensifies the binary of the two forms of intelligence: the inferior intelligence, or "the young child and the common man" (Rancière, 1991, p. 7), and the superior one (e.g., the master). The binary regresses into an entrenchment of inequality.

This issue calls to my mind the ways in which childhood art was studied in the early twentieth century, as seen in Goodenough's (1926) *Draw a Man Test* that allegedly produced evidence of differences in children's drawing capacities. The test was figured under the premise that it is natural for intelligences of children not to be equal. This supposed measurement of intelligence is the mere enactment of inequality; explicating differences in human development by labeling certain abilities as intelligent while others are not, which only manages to reaffirm the idea that intelligence is hierarchical. What Rancière contends does not suggest that all intelligences are the same, but that there is only one intelligence at work in all intellectual training (Rancière, 2010, p. 5). One intelligence, here, connotes that rather than a divisive and dichotomous status between intellectual capacities, it is the effort of will that has to be activated to activate the equally endowed intelligence of all people. Insofar as intelligence cannot be measured in isolation from what it produces (e.g., acts and effects) it is the manifestation of willingness that becomes visible.

The myth of explication evokes Paulo Freire's (2000) metaphor of the "banking model" of education, in which the teacher deposits knowledge into the students. After the initial deposit, the scope of action permitted to the students extends only to receiving, filing, and storing the deposit. Like the act of explication, the banking model assumes a strict hierarchical order in the classroom: the teacher acts (e.g., teaches, thinks, disciplines, delivers) and the students are acted upon (e.g., taught, thought about, listen, receive). The teacher possesses superior knowledge while the students know little or nothing; the teacher is an agentic person of sense whereas the students are merely objects to be acted upon. Therefore, the problematic pedagogical assumption of the students' mind as a blank slate persists (e.g., Locke's immanent child image[1]), and therefore explication justifies and is deeply engrained in every aspect of education, as well as any adult-child relationships that do nothing but hinder students from becoming active learners *and* teachers.

The logic and practice of explication is also problematic as it presumes a concealed *truth* that could only be uncovered by the master explicator. Rancière (1991) claims that "Truth is not told" (p. 60), but it is the arbitrariness of language that fragments it. In educational practice, however, it is too often the case that students are prevented from attending to this arbitrariness (i.e., prevented from questioning, being in conflict, or creating their own ways of learning). Considering language as a power structure, Rancière presents his agonistic perspective toward such explanatory discourse that aims to achieve truth. Instead, he presents the logic of "emancipation" as an opposite concept of stultification (Rancière, 2009a). Emancipation, to Rancière, is not simply about moving from a minority group to a majority group, but rather denotes a "rupture in the order of things" (Rancière, 2003, p. 219). In other words, it disrupts the configuration of the oppositional relationship of the one who dominates and the one who is subjected to domination.

In the case of Jacotot, both the master and students constituted an emancipatory experience by dissociating with their socially expected roles and attending to the encouragement to use their own intellectual capacities. Furthermore, in the case of children's drawing, the explicatory practice of studying children's art has traditionally meant seeking forms of reasoning and truth that align with a developmental model, merely perpetuating the deficit model of childhood (e.g., see Cannella, 1997; Matthews, 2008, 2009). Similar to Rancière's description of stultification, the deficit child model assumes the nature of the child as a configuration of deficits—missing capacities that adults generally have. Gareth Matthews (2008, 2009) argues that this model undervalues the fact that children are, for instance, better able to learn a foreign language, produce aesthetic artworks, or conceive philosophically interesting questions. The presumption, therefore, restricts the range and value of potential relationships between adults and children. In challenging this dominant idea, I suggest that an emancipatory practice attends to the alternative narratives of children's works and lives, looking into what might actually happen when the explicatory tendency is suspended.

The radical break between two forms of intelligence does not remove the schoolmaster's *will*. The ignorant teacher may not impose his knowledge but manifests instead the authority to instigate the intellectual capacity of students. For Rancière, the method of equality is a method of will, which stimulates the intellect and comes before intelligence. The students learned not by the teacher's explication, but "propelled by their own desire" (Rancière, 1991, p. 12). And, likewise, the teacher actuated his will to leave his intelligence out of the picture. The only thing that had been established between Jacotot and the students was a will for attentiveness and a will to conduct a search, constituting "a pure relationship of will to will" (Rancière, 1991, p. 13). The students conducted the translation of the foreign language text by activating their own will, and the schoolmaster, cognizant of what remains unknown to the students and also the ways to make it knowable, also willingly put aside the dominant role of explication.

The wills operated to discover the thing in common, which is the intelligence of the book *Télémaque* that served as "the egalitarian intellectual link between master and student" (Rancière, 1991, p. 13). The book functioned not only as a primary source of knowledge but also as a site for the knowledge to emerge within the engagement with it. It was a mediator that produced something different, which Rancière describes elsewhere as the "third thing":

> In the logic of emancipation, between the ignorant schoolmaster and the emancipated novice there is always a third thing—a book or some other piece of writing—alien to both and to which they can refer to verify in common what the pupil has seen, what she says about it and what she thinks of it.
>
> (Rancière, 2011, pp. 14–15)

In Jacotot's class, the "third thing" is not the vision of the master's knowledge or inspiration to the students, but something whose meaning is not owned by anybody—it exists between them (Rancière, 2011). Ignorance, accompanied with the student's and Jacotot's will to learn, and *Télémaque* functioning as the third thing, therefore, produced intellectual emancipation. It was the logic of action being reformulated on the basis of subverting the traditional roles assigned to the role of a master and student.

Rancière's Practice of Ignorance

Rancière's elaboration of intellectual equality and emancipation in *The Ignorant Schoolmaster* is neither an imaginary nor utopian concept conceived by a thinker from a distanced viewpoint. Instead, Rancière has internalized and practiced equality himself, as the story of Jacotot and his students closely aligns with Rancière's personal break from his own mentor, Louis Althusser (1918–90). Being a student of Althusser at the École Normale Supérieure in the 1960s, Rancière was initially interested in traditional Marxism. He soon followed Althusser's unorthodox Marxism which represented a different view from his own previous understanding of Marx. Rancière co-authored *Reading Capital* with Althusser, which, along with Althusser's *For Marx*, thereby helped to define the field of structuralist Marxism. However, Rancière broke away from his mentor as Althusser began to distance himself from political mobilizations during and after the events of May 1968, including the famous student uprising led by students that occurred in May and June of that year.

This event influenced many French thinkers such as Gilles Deleuze, Jacques Derrida, and Michel Foucault in strikingly diverse ways. Committed to his membership in the French Communist Party, Althusser accepted its conservative response to the uprising and refused to support the strikes or demonstrations. Many of Althusser's students who had previously viewed his ideas as a critical new development in revolutionary politics bitterly rejected Althusser's mentorship, thinking that he was unable to act beyond the dictates of the party bureaucrats.

Rancière also witnessed that Althusser stood for the power of the professors during the creation of the philosophy department of Paris VIII, a program designed to teach theoretical practice as it *should* be taught. Rancière was against this program and criticized the "dogmatism of theory and on the position of scholarly knowledge [Althusser's students] had adopted" (Rancière, 2017, p. 117). To Rancière, it seemed paradoxical that Althusser's theory of a discourse "pretended to speak the truth about what political and social actors practiced, but which these same actors did not, or could not, think on their own" (Rancière, 2017, p. 71). It was Althusser's preaching of a "philosophy of order" that "anaesthetized the revolt against the bourgeoisie" (Rockhill, 2013, p. xii) and thus widened the gap between his theory and reality. As such, Rancière broke with his mentor and began to critically re-examine the socio-political and historical forces in operation in the production of theory (Rockhill, 2013).

Rancière did this first by writing *Althusser's Lesson* (1974) in which, through a radical yet unique voice, he explains the theoretical and political distance separating his position from the Althusserian Marxist position. Rancière rejects the elitism of Althusser that insisted upon the gap separating the "universe of scientific cognition" from that of "ideological (mis) recognition" of the common masses (Rancière, 2013a, p. 65). Instead, he rewrites the genealogy of Marxism to examine the difference between Marxism and what could have been an alternative workers' tradition. It insists on the urgency of time that is full of possibilities to present Marxism as a way of thinking an imminent victory. That is, as Rancière returns to the original thoughts of Marxism, the target of his critique in *Althusser's Lesson* is not so much on Althusser, but Althusserian Marxism, or Althusserianism (Rancière, 2017). Skeptical of Marxist-inspired criticism that seeks to uncover hidden or underlying power structures, Rancière's own theory is grounded in his criticism of the critical theory, claiming that the problematization of the ideological process of assigning bodies to think and act in particular ways was essential. With this claim, intellectual equality became central to his philosophy.

It was not only Althusser's political standpoint in the 1960s but his pedagogical practice that Rancière denounced. The depiction of stultification in *The Ignorant Schoolmaster,* in fact, echoes Althusser's method of teaching Marxism to his students to a certain extent. Similar to Freire's (2000) description of the "banking model," Althusser, as caricatured in Rancière's book *The Flesh of Words: The Politics of Writing* (2004a), used the method of "symptomal reading" wherein the teacher would leave particular words absent in parentheses for the students to fill out, and the students would in turn restore the sentences left incomplete by figuring out the designated word. As such, this work of filling in the blank of a missing signifier, which Althusser called "dotted lines," was believed to be the method of effectively producing knowledge. This method parallels to how children were taught to draw in public schools in late nineteenth and early twentieth century in Austria, before Franz Cizek discovered "child art" (Viola, 1936): in school art classes, children were asked to connect dots with straight lines to create geometric shapes and figures, and as the age advanced, only the gap between the dots were further apart (Viola, 1936). Both Althusser and nineteenth-century school teachers in Austria used methods that functioned to verify that the student understands the lesson correctly and knows how to apply what has been taught. A hierarchy of knowledge was created in that there were proper, unquestionable answers or ways of doing that fit within in the parenthesis, as well as an inevitable dependency on the teacher. The dotted lines in Althusser's teaching were "the presence of the teacher in his absence" (Rancière, 2004a, p. 134) that gauged—if not haunted—the students to submit to the hierarchy by inserting the one-right-answer. Perhaps Rancière was attracted to the story of Jacotot and his students for his empathy with the opposite case, of stultification, the presence of a hierarchical knowledge in his learning of Marxism prior to his break with Althusser.

Nonetheless, Rancière acknowledges that even in symptomal reading the students were in some ways allowed to construct the ideas for themselves, as he mentioned in his interview with political philosopher Peter Hallward that

Althusser "taught very little [content]" (Rancière, 2003, p. 194). This insinuates that although the symptomal reading method aligned with the pedagogy of stultification, Althusser's approach to having his students read and think about Marxism does not entirely overlap with the master explicator who merely transmits knowledge and thus reinforces inequality. In other words, students were still able to find room to activate their will to learn and construct meanings. It is this gray area that troubled Rancière; his idea of pedagogy rests on the basis of intellectual equality, not one which only somewhat allow free thinking, nor one which try to produce equality as a result of education.

Concerning how Rancière posits in *The Aesthetic Unconscious* (2009b) that critical theory could not have happened without certain aesthetic projects (e.g., Romanticism and post-Kantian idealism) emerging as a precedence, which resulted in a redistribution of the sensible between thinking and feeling, I suspect that Rancière's experience of Althusser's pedagogy affected him to conceive the aesthetic domain of pedagogy. As such, Rancière's radical reconceptualization of equality emerged from his own studentship and response against some of the ideologies of the Left, along with his critical reflection on the nature of pedagogical practices, that imagines a pedagogy on the basis of emancipation.

Emancipation and Equality

Then, what is emancipation? Etymologically, emancipation is to give away ownership: *e-* (variant of *ex-*) means "out or away" and *mancipum* means "ownership."[2] Historically, it originated from Roman law, as it referred to the freeing of a son or wife from the legal authority of the father of the family. This implies that the aim of the person to be emancipated is to become independent as a result of the act of emancipation. What Rancière argues through *The Ignorant Schoolmaster* is, however, that a student does not attain independence by achieving an adult or a master status but by separating from the master's intelligence and will. That is, if stultification is one intelligence (e.g., the student) being subordinated to the other intelligence (e.g., the teacher), emancipation is when the two intelligences become separate and independent from each other. For example, in Jacotot's experimental teaching of *Télémaque,* the students were connected to Jacotot's will, rather than his intelligence. In this connection, a process also takes place by which one would conceive her human dignity, measure her own intellectual capacity, and determine how to use it (Rancière, 1991). To reiterate what emancipation means in Rancièrian terms, it is not about one's status moving toward a majority group, but instead a deliberate rupture in the common sense.

The essence of emancipatory, particularly in education, is not so much about unveiling ideologies or the knowledge transfer between the teacher and the student, but more so about those who have no part in verifying effects of equality. Educational scholar Gert Biesta (2008) conceives a new logic of emancipation by comparing it with an old notion of emancipation. The old notion premises the presence of a fundamental inequality, where emancipation is something done to somebody and requires an intervention by someone who is not dependent on the power that needs to be overcome. As such, paradoxically, the act of emancipation requires an intervention of the emancipator as if a gift could be given from them; this speaks to the fundamental inequality in education insofar as "emancipation marks the moment when and the process through which the (dependent) child becomes an (independent) adult" (Biesta, 2008, p. 169). In contrast, the new logic of emancipation no longer relies on this relationship of dependency. Biesta draws from Foucault (1975, 1991) and Rancière (1989, 1991) to inform this proposal:

> People need not wait until their emancipators tell them that they can move; they can make the move *right here* and *right now*. This also shows that new emancipation starts from the assumption of equality, in that everyone is considered to be able to make the move. This is not to suggest that society is equal. But what it aims to do is to take away from the logic of emancipation the idea that there is a fundamental, almost ontological inequality that only can be overcome through the interventions of the emancipator.
>
> (Biesta, 2008, p. 175, my emphasis)

Further, continuing the Rancièrian orientation, Biesta (2008) states that in the new logic of emancipation people's experiences and appearances are taken seriously, as opposed to the old emancipation where only those who have parts in the society can have valid experiences. In other words, while the old logic of emancipation only validated the voices who were regarded as legitimate beings within the distribution of the sensible, the new logic opens up possibilities for *all* people to enact emancipation right here and right now on the basis of intellectual equality.

If put into the context of early childhood education and early childhood art education, producing a new logic of emancipation would entail assuming equality within our every interaction with children, right here and right now, dissociating with the habitual teaching that often reproduces stultification or the myth of pedagogy. As I proceed with my argument in practicing the assumption of intellectual equality in early childhood spaces, I am also aware of how unsettling it might be to think about equal positions between adults and young children—or more specifically, the teacher and young children—if taken verbatim. It is often misunderstood that the purpose of contending with equality is to completely undo inequality and render equal opportunities or power for everyone. However, undoing inequality is not only impossible—at least in our modern society—but also not the purpose of arguing for equality. In fact, no two humans can have absolutely equal opportunity unless they are identically the same person. Moreover, it is also not to confuse equality with equity, the social distribution of fairness. Whereas equity is given, "posed as a project done to or for classifiable social actors," Rancière's concept of intellectual equality emphasizes its essential practice as "something than can be tested, tried, and ongoingly renewed" (Thumlert, 2015, p. 126). Equality, therefore, rests on willful acts to see what becomes visible when the assumption and practice is set forth.

Here, the *doing* of equality is not to confuse it with something that can be achieved at the end. Rancièrian equality is not so much about gradually accomplishing equality as a result of a provocation, but rather something that is "either asserted at the outset or is irremediably lost" (Tanke, 2011, p. 36). It is the initial assumption of and ongoing practice of verifying equality to begin with that produces possibilities of an equal status. This in turn produces affects that are different from the relationship or pedagogical practice which don't assume equality in the first place.

For Rancière, the problem is not about proving that all intelligences are equal, but instead "seeing what can be done under that supposition" (Rancière, 1991, p. 46). In other words, we ought to focus on the *effects* of equality that emerge when deploying the presupposition of equality and willfully practicing it. Inasmuch as I view the deficit model images and realities surrounding children as a haunting portrayal of inequality, the Rancièrian idea of equality offers productive ways to think about the approaches and ethics of researching with children as an endeavor to ease the haunts in early childhood art education.

Politics: The Re-distribution of the Sensible

As seen in the *Ignorant Schoolmaster*, when one assumes equality it functions as "a destabilizing force which allows those invoking it to assert themselves as political agents" (Tanke, 2011, p. 36). As an opponent of the normalization of sensible hierarchies, Rancière uses the word "politics" or "political" as an activity that turns on equality as its principle, rather than to subscribe to the liberal idea that politics occur upon a rational debate between pre-established groups divided by interests.

It is a provocative idea that suggests an alternative viewpoint on politics beyond the conventional definition of politics as governmental exercise of power. To further investigate Rancière's critical analysis of politics, I find Oliver Davis's (2010) emphasis on four main points of Rancièrian politics to be a useful framework, especially to clarify a somewhat broad account of politics. For Davis, the four points are: (1) politics as an opposition to "police," (2) Rancière's structural account of democratic politics, (3) the theory of political "subjects" and "subjectivation," and (4) the aesthetic dimensions to politics (pp. 74–100). As Davis (2010) admits, this sequential presentation of politics may seem artificial because all four aspects are inextricably interwoven. However, setting the four elements as pillars has been the most helpful approach for me to understand the grandiose concept of politics as a whole.

Politics as an Opposition to "the Police"

Politics occur as an opposition to the *police,* which prevails as a distribution of the sensible that defines the territory one should occupy and, accordingly, the expected activity of the allocated position. Rancière's "police" plays on the Greek word *polis,* which Alan Badiou stated, is to designate "those distributions erected in order to support the selective accountings" (Tanke, 2011, p. 43) of a social community. In fact, Rancière's notion of "politics" reserves space for alternative visions, and furthermore, turns over what is normally understood as politics as "the police":

> Rancière claims to be drawing here on an older and wider sense of the term "police" than the familiar one of a repressive organ of state, one closer to that identifies by Foucault in seventeenth- and eighteenth-century writings as almost synonymous with the social order in its eternity ... The opposition between "the police" and "politics" and the remaining of most of what is normally thought of as politics as "policing" is a *twisting* of the ordinary usage of both terms which blurs their "proper" meanings and *dramatizes* the conflict between them.
>
> (Davis, 2010, p. 76, original emphasis)

As Rancière intends the resonances of coercion and repression often associated with the police, in a broader sense, it is important to note here that there is another, more historical reference to the term, one that has been analyzed by Michel Foucault. The Foucauldian police refers to the concept of the "early" police (Foucault, 2007) emergent in France and Germany during the seventeenth and eighteenth century, which is set of practices and inscription of rationality as an expression of the new attitude toward life, that seek both to utilize and to maintain the population of a state. This type of policing is concerned with the demographics, health, and safety of a population, with a purpose to contribute optimally to the welfare of the state. The current state of mainstream politics has relevance of this association. Although it is not only the state but also corporate elites who benefit from the population's stability, the general idea of police remains much the same.

Politics is a particular type of event that emerges with respect to these police orders, when that "part of those who have no part [*la part des sans-part*]" (Rancière, 1999, p. 11) counter the distribution of the sensible that excludes them. The term "part of those without part" is used by Rancière to discuss the social reality resulted by the police and the people who are excluded in the distribution of the sensible. For example, it has been historically thought that politics entails the task of managing the struggle between the rich and the poor. However, Rancière thinks differently:

> The struggle between the rich and the poor ... is the actual institution of politics itself. There is politics when there is a part of those who have no part, a part or party of the poor. Politics does not happen just because the poor oppose the rich. It is the other way around: politics (that is, the interruption of the simple effects of domination by the rich) causes the poor to exist as an entity.
>
> (Rancière, 1999, p. 11)

Politics, or political subjectivation, emerges out of a paradoxical attempt by those who are considered less-than, or not recognized as equals, venture to insist upon their equality despite their assigned part. Thinking about the politics of "those who have no part" invokes the reality of children as having no part in citizenship, research, and even within their everyday lives, being heavily dominated by the power of adults. In this sense, the very fact that children are regarded as having no part *is* politics, causing them to exist as a political community. Thus, politics occurs when the natural, normalized order of power is dismantled by the community of those who have no part. In other words, the politics of the community of *sans-part* is a *re*-distribution of the sensible.

Rancière's Account of Democratic Politics

What Rancière contends through arguing the re-distribution of the sensible is *demos*, the "subject" of politics. As a concept from which Rancière's "part of those who have no part [*la part des sans-part*]" originated, Aristotle's notion of the *demos* comes into play for illustrating the definition: the men of no position, those who "had no part in anything" (Rhodes, 1984, as cited in Rancière, 1999, p. 9). Demos, in this regard, is assumed to be silenced in the arrangement structured by the police. Yet it also holds the immanent power to render truly political instances by interrupting the public scene, in spite of the assigned role given by so-called democratic forms of policing. Rancière (1999) views this hierarchy of inequality created by the police as the fundamental "wrong" *[Le Tort]*[3] of the sans-part's nonrecognition. Therefore, the essence of democratic politics exists in opposition to the police, especially when the bodies (e.g., those who have no part) deliberately process "dis-identification, or the undoing of the bonds tying bodies to specific places, of the various forms of privatization of speech or emotion" (Corcoran, 2015, p. 5). Returning to Jacotot and the students' dissociation from the traditional roles and identities of master and student, politics exists when a community opposes the distribution of the sensible for rendering a community of equality.

This idea of disagreeing with the natural order is what Rancière (2015) calls "dissensus," which emphasizes all people's equality and the expression of original forms of identity. Being at the heart of politics, the act of dissensus entails the manifestation of a radical displacement and emancipation from the ways that police distributed orders and partitioned bodies as an alleged consensus. For Rancière, consensus does entail disputes and conflicts. But these types of conflicts are already part of the common without allowing room for confrontation and "dispute over the existence of the dispute" (Rancière, 1999, p. 55). In other words, dissensuality is essential for political subjects to attend to emancipation and thus practice the assumption of equality.

On a similar connotation, Dennis Atkinson (2018) uses the term "disobedience" to refer to the practices that run counter to the dominant, established frameworks in education. Atkinson thereby suggests heterogeneous approaches to existing patterns. Such approaches can potentiate new transformations of a world of coexistence. Atkinson (2018) writes that disobedience should not be thought of as "being awkward or rebellious simply for the sake of it, but in terms of an event of non-compliance that opens up new ways of thinking and acting" (p. 195). This is why Rancière's politics is a democratic politics; it is a contingently egalitarian practice that fractures the distribution of the sensible where it governs "normal" experience.

Political Subjects and Subjectivation

The process in which individuals stray away from their natural assigned partitions within the police order, that is, the struggle to claim their existence as political subjects, is what Rancière refers to as "subjectivation"[4] (Rancière, 1992, 2013a). Tanke (2011) writes, "If dissensus creates the stage of politics, one can claim that political subjectivation establishes its players, provided we do not separate the two processes" (p. 66). That is, the agents who enact dissensus attain political subjectivation via the tension and struggle in which such dissensuality results.

Rancière's subjectivation functions as an integral element of politics, in contrast to the historical account of the subject in French philosophy. The creation of subjectivity has been regarded as the imposition of an ideological state apparatus (e.g., Althusser's analysis of subject) or the self-constitution as subjects via power/knowledge (Foucault, 1975). Contrary to these ideas, Rancière contends in his article "Politics, identification, and subjectivization" that political subjectivation is "made out of the difference between the voice and the body, the interval between identities" and therefore a political subject is situated at "an interval or a gap: being *together* to the extent that we are in *between*—between names, identities, cultures, and so on" (Rancière, 1992, p. 62, original italics). It is an enactment of equality whereby those of no part divert from their given identity to deal with the "wrong," to struggle for their existence, which puts them in a liminal space between the assigned and the "subject" identity.

Davis (2010) adopts Rancière's three main characteristics of the process of subjectivation: (1) an argumentative demonstration, (2) a theatrical dramatization, and (3) a heterologic disidentification (p. 84). The first characteristic of the *argumentative demonstration* in political subjectivation recalls Rancière's insistence on the *practical* verification of equality. Practicality functions as a core value in Rancièrian equality because it consists of struggles that involve language and action-oriented arguments rather than relying on formal declarations of equality in legal or constitutional documents. Yet Rancière does believe that such documents could "serve as the basis for a practical verification of that equality, as part of a logical, argumentative, demonstration of the sort enacted by the tailors" (Davis, 2010, p. 85).

The second aspect of subjectivation, a *theatrical dramatization*, means that the process of subjectivation is spectacular, as politics transforms the normalized space into a space for the appearance of a subject (Rancière, 2001). Referring to Hallward's (2006, 2009) description of Rancièrian politics as "theatrocracy," Davis (2010) writes that theater is linked to democracy insofar as actors being themselves yet simultaneously being someone else allows them to have a political existence in addition to their own identity:

> political subjectivation resembles acting because both involve the ruse of pretending you are something you are not in order to become it: for the *sans-*

part this means pretending you are already equal participants in the political process from which in fact, by virtue of the "wrong" of the miscount, you are excluded. ... politics for Rancière is, in a broader sense, creative or constructive in that it involves not only the manifestation of a new subject but the construction of a common space or "scene" of relationality which did not exist previously.

(Davis, 2010, pp. 86–87, original italics)

Situating this idea of theatrocratic politics in the case of children as having no part, the political subjectivation of children would involve a pretense of the other—the adult. Specifically, the process of subjectivation demands that children construct and practice as a new subject that is distinct from their given identity, as well as to create a "scene" within the common space that highlights their existence, to make themselves visible. This idea of making a "scene" within a shared space makes possible how particular events in children's everyday spaces (e.g., classrooms) could be considered as political events. In fact, this is the main question of my study—to study how children might create a political scene in their everyday lives as a means to voice and legitimize themselves as political subjects.

The third dimension of political subjectivation, the *heterologic disidentification*, is the idea that political subjectivation entails an "impossible identification" with a different subject or otherness in general (Davis, 2010, p. 87). As mentioned above, the process of political subjectivation involves not only declaring an identity but, more importantly, dissenting the identity given by the police. It is the process of subjects being placed in the gap between the identities. This is what heterologic disidentification means: the identities and social roles create temporary, unsettling, and entangled subject positions. Considering how children have been hauntingly pushed to the part of having "no part" by the police, in order for children to be political subjects, the process entails a dissociation of their assigned partition and assertion of the other identity. Here, what I think of as asserting the "other" identity is not merely wishing to become the adult figure; rather, if children attend to political subjectivation, it would be to declare the *logic* of being an adult, to have the same legibility and sensibility (e.g., to be seen and heard). In fact, children have always been heterogeneous beings: children have been living in the in-between world—between the world of their own and that of adults' (Corsaro, 2015) and between nature and culture (e.g., Haraway,1991; Prout, 2011). This innate hybridity of childhood provides the foundation for children to be political subjects, if children disidentify themselves from their expected social roles, thus asserting the identity of the legible other.

The Aesthetic Dimensions to Politics

The fourth characteristic of politics is what makes Rancière's idea of politics unique: the *aesthetic dimension* of it. Aesthetics, here, does not mean beauty or art theories, but the perception of the sensible. As Rancière (2013a) describes it, politics "revolves around what is seen and what can be said about it, around who has the ability to see and the talent to speak, around the properties of spaces and the possibilities of time" (p. 8). More specifically, when those of *sans-part* voice themselves, there is a tendency that such utterances are not heard as a rational argument that contains valid meaning. It is more likely to be unheard and disregarded because that is how the police put them into the partition of having no part, no voice, and no visibility. Therefore, the process of political subjectivation brings those with no part into visible and audible beings—it is a process whereby invisibility comes into presence and noise becomes language. This is a form of re-partitioning the sensible and reconfiguring what defines the common of the community, rendering the possibility of the invisible being visible and the unheard being heard. In this regard, the distribution of the sensible does not remain as binaries but rather works performatively within the time and space of those who were subject to being partitioned within the logic of inequality.

As such, for Rancière, politics is not the governmental practice or the struggle for power but a configuration of a specific space—the organization of a particular sphere of experience—of objects posited as common, as pertaining to a common sense, and putting forward arguments about them (Rancière, 2004b). Politics troubles the habitually accepted distribution of the sensible in our everyday lives that, for example, put the rich or poor, male or female, old or young, into their "proper" occupation and accordingly into one's place. Politics, therefore, is a contingently egalitarian practice that fractures the distribution of the sensible, which, as previously described, is just one more annoying way of governing "normal" experience and pretending that we can somehow "attain" a sense of equality, but of course, we can only *assume* one. The aesthetic character of politics, therefore, brings attention to all people's equality and the expression of original forms of identity by highlighting the political subjects' dissensual acts.

Thus far I have described four characteristics of Rancière's politics as the manifestation of a radical displacement and emancipation from the ways that police partition bodies. Though the aesthetic dimension of politics discussed in the last section was more about the sensible rather than the arts, Rancière does in fact explore the notion of aesthetics within the artistic realm. Creating a synonymous idea between politics and aesthetics, he views the historical account of art in three regimes and defines one of them as an "aesthetic regime." The next section explores the specific connotations of Rancièrian aesthetics and how the concept could be used throughout this book.

Aesthetics: The Regime of Equality

Continuing with Rancière's characterization of the distribution of the sensible, historically, aesthetics has been a discursive regime of art in which order(s) of the police govern more or less desirable qualities in art production and art appreciation. However, like politics, art emerged as an egalitarian suspension of the hierarchical modes of representation that was prevalent in artistic practices until the late eighteenth century. The identity of art was shifted in the end of eighteenth and the beginning of the nineteenth century by the "aesthetic revolution," which was a rethinking of what is to count as a work of art. As such, how Rancière uses the term *aesthetics* is quite different from the everyday use of it: to Rancière, aesthetics does not refer to a theory of beauty, sensibility, or taste. Instead, "the property of being art is no longer given by the criteria of technical perfection but is ascribed to a specific form of sensory apprehension" (Rancière, 2004b, p. 29). Here, specificity entails the aesthetic experience that assumes equality between the artwork and viewers. It is the political capacity of art of that Rancière focuses on, especially on its immanent ability to alter and divert from the distribution of the sensible through the creation of experiences that counter the common sense. Art is constitutive of recognition, meaning, and signification.

The Three Regimes

Rancière's re-thinking of aesthetics is achieved by glancing through the history of art, arguing that art is political inasmuch as it never exists as an abstraction, but always conditional to the way it is perceived in different historical periods or regimes (Rancière, 2013a, 2013b, 2015). He conceptualizes three regimes in which art has been primarily situated: the *ethical, representational*, and *aesthetic* regime. First, in the ethical regime, as exemplified by Plato's *Republic*,[5] works of art lack autonomy; for example, a sculpture is measured against the question of truthfulness and adequacy between subject matter and representation. Artworks are assimilated into the question of images' origin—and thus their truth—as well as their purpose, their uses, and their effects of the individuals and the community. Truth, here, is consistent with the "explanatory order" Rancière (1991) described as a fixed endpoint that precludes emancipatory practices, which in fact functioned in this regime to preclude artisans from having any creative flexibility in their practice of producing works of imitation. Hence, the ethical regime is preoccupied with the truth-value of images and its morality.

Second, in the representational regime, art is no longer subject to the rules of truth or utility, but identified within the distinction of *mimesis* (imitation) and *poiesis* (the way of doing). This regime is also called "poetic" because, by breaking away from the ethical regime, it identifies art within the specific criteria of identification, the ways of doing and making (e.g., painting, drawing, sculpting). An interesting point made by Rancière (2004b) is that mimesis is not so much about the obligation to the resemblance, defined by skill and practice, but rather the divisive principle in human activities that renders objects to be subsumed under particular concepts and qualities. It separated what is considered art and what is not. Therefore, this representative regime is classified under the hierarchy of social and political occupations, the hierarchy of genres corresponding to the dignity of their subject matter, and the very primacy of the art of speaking in actuality (Rancière, 2013a).

While the two former regimes of art were bound to the service of moral, social, and political function, the third regime, the *aesthetic* regime of art, contrasts with those regimes whereby it identifies art in the singular and liberates art from the rules, genres, expectations about form and matter, or any hierarchy of the arts. Art now belongs to a heterogeneous sensorium that is liberated from the previous normative network art served. It no longer requires a narrative of social significance or a system of meaning in order to be called art. If the former regimes identified art by the law of mimesis in its strict relation between *poiesis* and *aesthesis*—the ways of being affected by the ways of doing—in the aesthetic regime of art the link between the doing and being is divorced, thus opening up the possibility for art to address itself, inviting anyone to create, use, gaze, and appreciate it in any situation. It is a particular regime for identifying and reflecting on the arts as "a mode of articulation between ways of doing and making, their corresponding forms of visibility, and possible ways of thinking about their relationships" (Rancière, 2013a, p. 4). The aesthetic regime can be identified with the interpretive space in which the artwork demands that one does not merely observe, but interpret, based on the relationship between the apparent and the concealed.

Genuine aesthetics entail active thinking—the ways of doing and making that break with the general distribution of ways of doing and making. Rancière (2013b) reworks this notion of "aesthetics" concerning the sense of *aesthetic*, an autonomous, innovative activity of experience that could not be categorized under logic, reason, or morality. In other words, it is not the autonomy of the *work of art*, but the autonomy of one's *experience* in relation to art that is emphasized. It is a matter of thinking the complicated link between autonomy and heteronomy between art becoming life and life becoming art (Rancière, 2002) in its ignorance to the subject matter and the distinction between art and nonart. The experience of the aesthetic challenges how the world is organized and constructed, which entails the possibility of changing or redistributing the world (Rancière, 2015).

Though disparately unique, the aesthetic regime cannot be understood apart from its relation to the preceding aesthetic presuppositions. For example, in *The Aesthetic Unconscious* (2009b), Rancière complicates the relation between the sensible and the intellectual where he discusses Freud's appropriation of the Oedipus myth, claiming that "Freudian thought of the unconscious is only possible on the basis of this regime of thinking about art and the idea of thought that is immanent to it" (p. 7). He contrasts the conception of Kantian aesthetic with the view of the sensible found in the writings of the Schlegels, Schelling, and Hegel in order to reveal the aesthetic presuppositions that resulted in the development of psychoanalysis. As such, the aesthetic regime of art is only possible on the basis of the rejection toward the distribution of the sensible in the poetic regime, albeit continuously remains in tension between being specifically art and bringing together other forms of activity and being.

Dissensus as Aesthetic

Art and politics consist of forms of *dis-sensus*—a process of re-ordering of the senses (Rancière, 2015). Rancière views modern society as a time of consensus, which does not indicate that everyone approves all the public policies, "but rather that there is a general agreement that the partition of the sensible and its distribution of roles is a reasonable one, and that there is no reasonable alternative to it" (May, 2010, para. 7). In order for there to be a politics and aesthetics, dissensus is essential, one that reconfigures the forms of visibility and intelligibility thus intervene in the distribution of the sensible. Political and artistic practices, in other words, involve a mode of emancipation in which "bodies are torn from their assigned places, and exhibit verbal competencies and emotional capabilities they are not supposed to have by virtue of the space and time they occupy" (Corcoran, 2015, pp. 4–5). Anything can be politics and aesthetics if it overthrows the logic of hierarchies that determine the status of, for example, artistic practices and the very nature of their sensory experiences. Philosopher Todd May describes how dissensual actions come about within a community of *sans-part*:

> Such action, if it is political, is going to be collective rather than individual. It will concern a group of people (or a subset of that group) who have been presupposed unequal by a particular hierarchical order, as well as those in solidarity with them, acting as though they were indeed equal to those above them in the order, and thus disrupting the social order itself. What are disrupted are not only the power arrangements of the social order, but, and more deeply, the perceptual and epistemic underpinnings of that order, the

obviousness and naturalness that attaches to the order. Such a disruption is what Rancière calls a dissensus.

(May, 2010, para. 4)

This is why Rancière's idea of politics and aesthetics compels me to think about it side by side to children's art practices, as it opens up possibilities for considering children's artistic experiences as legitimate ones. Throughout the history of art education, children's art has always been policed by adults' order and control, under the premise that childhood art and its development is "obvious" or "natural." Thus, it is this notion of politics and aesthetics, and more specifically the synonymity between the two, that demands we think through children's art.

Rancière's work on the relation between art, education, and politics, however, is quite perplexing (Lewis, 2012, p. 7). For example, there's a conflation of education with the arts of the aesthetic regime. A conflation of education with political subjectivation in the form of the "ignorant citizen" (Biesta, 2011), produces a concept that shifts our understanding of education from a process that socializes newcomers into existing social and political orders to education as an event that constitutes new political subjectivities. Moreover, some might argue that Rancière's pedagogy that bases on the story of Jacotot in the nineteenth century is quite untimely, as modern education no longer follows the educational model of centralized knowledge. Despite these reckonings, I maintain my stance that finds Rancière's ideas relevant to the study of childhood art practices; young children's status as "less-than" beings subject to adult control have not demonstrated a drastic change during the past century. Continuing this thought, the next chapter discusses the distribution of the sensible in our understandings of childhood and childhood art with a particular focus on historically sustained accounts on the deficient model predicated on developmental psychology.

2

Ghostly Matters of Childhood and Childhood Art

Admittedly, police and politics may not be the most delightful topic to discuss in the study of childhood art, but it is certainly one of the most important discussions for recognizing the policed reality of children's art. Policing not only occurs on the personal level, but, more importantly, in the *history* of child art and art education. Though history tends to associate with notions of the past, where events diminish to the realm of "old" or "gone," it nonetheless heavily influences the doings and beings of our present time. Drawing on Rancière's (1999) idea that some police order is inevitable and one cannot exist in a purely free realm outside of a police order, this chapter is on the premise that certain theories and images of childhood remain as ghosts. As such, this chapter examines how a police order persists in the study of childhood and childhood art by, first, unpacking this ghost, and second, looking at childhood images in their specificity, in order to understand the reality children live in as well as to suggest that we attend to the particularities of children's lives.

In thinking about this out-of-joint time, Jacques Derrida's (1994) idea of "hauntology" in his book *Spectres of Marx* provides insight for construing history being out of linear order of time: Hauntology denotes that the temporal, historical, and epistemological traces converge with the presence of being— the ontology. Derrida uses the plural spectres (or specters) intentionally, given that Marxism embraces diverse interpretation and revision upon the changing cultural conditions. Considering how these ghosts of Marx continue to haunt the paradigm of Western liberal democracy's supposed "triumph" over communism, Derrida describes how there is neither a beginning nor an end to history:

> Given that a *revenant* is always called upon to come and to come back, the
> thinking of the spectre, contrary to what good sense leads us to believe,
> signals toward the future. It is a thinking of the past, a legacy that can come
> only from that which has not yet arrived—from the *arrivant*[1] itself.
>
> (Derrida, 1994, p. 196, original italics)

It is the peculiar presence that is no longer or not-yet present, yet inviting the
past and future to converge.

Derrida's deconstructive structure of the play between the present and
absent is, in fact, distinct from Rancière's perspective on time and history, as
he sees the present as a sensible universe constructed from a/the moment in
the past, a holistic view rather than as a means of understanding the present.
This is not to say that the past is gone, but to avoid the past being in service to
understanding the present; when Rancière reflects on moments of the past, it
functions as a means "to destabilize it, to take away some of its obviousness"
(Rancière, 2016, p. 107). Nevertheless, Rancière (2011) admits that Derrida's
notion of hauntology addresses similar problems that Rancière confronts, for
example, how we perceive the distribution of the sensible. However, Rancière's
position is that Derrida oversubstantializes the identity of the inexistence, or
the presence of the absent. Although my thoughts align with most of Rancière's
theories throughout this book, it is the history of child art where I divert to
agree with Derrida's notion of hauntology for its effectiveness to understand
the elusive power that continues to influence children's art making today.
If opening up the idea of hauntings with my experience at the art hagwon
was more of a broader, allegorical thinking, here I use spectrality beyond
metaphors and narratives to undertake a substantive study of historical shifts
that concerns children's art.

Then, what does the ghost look like in the history of childhood art? More
specifically, what do they do to children? The historical account of children's
art cannot be discussed without also addressing how the study of childhood
has been informed and perpetuated by a deficit discourse that regards children
as "less-than." For example, psychologists and medical professionals have
bound children to a framework that positions them as less-developed in
relation to older members of the population (i.e., adults) (James et al., 1998),
and sociologists and philosophers have regarded children as less-than in

terms of their citizenship (Cohen, 2005; Marshall, 1950; Moosa-Mitha, 2005). As a result, children have continued to be vieweded as less-than adult—an understanding merely on their deficiency compared to the adult population. As such, the assumption that children are less capable than adults persisted as a ghost in the study of children's art, where children have been, and still are, considered less-than artists. This underpinning discourse also implies that children are a group of bodies not capable of having proper aesthetics, craftsmanship, culture and all the other aspects "adult" artists might embrace.

To use hauntology as part of continuing the discussion on children's art is to make it a place where I interrogate the constructed idea of child art in relation to the past, examine the elusive assumptions of the present, and explore the lines that may be drawn in the future. A ghost is a tradition inherited from the past, yet always to return, always to come, within the disjointed time. In looking into the past of the field of art education, the discourse of child art has a long history of categorizing children's drawings on the basis of age (e.g., developmental stage theories): whereby drawings are assumed to be a natural artifact of childhood, unaffected by culture, and distinctively innocent compared to those of adults. Therefore, the ghosts in child art are the notion that, on the basis of biomedical and sociological deficit models, children require adults' approval, guidance, or explication to "properly" make art in the "right" direction toward development.

Relatedly, I suspect Rancière would agree that the conception of child(ren) and childhood has been haunted by the predominant philosophies, power, and interests of adults as a constructed "plot" (Rancière, 2016), one that has been bound to specific knowledge systems and thus subjugated to the generalizable as part of the distribution of the sensible. These classifications established upon adults' beliefs and ideas that often decontextualize the child employ the deterministic scale used for the examination and evaluation of child art. It is the criteria of "biomedical designation of *age* and the aesthetic principles associated with *visual realism*, against which the competencies of children and their drawing are interpreted" (Schulte, 2018, p. 223, original emphasis). Though this plot continues to haunt children and the field of art education today, it also offers possibilities to reimagine and redistribute the sensible. In fact, as briefly mentioned in Chapter 1, Rancière (2009b) provides an example of the past haunting the present yet producing possibilities of the repartitioning of the sensible in *The Aesthetic Unconscious*, where he posits that critical theory was only possible because of preceding aesthetic projects, such as Romanticism. The unconscious structurings of the senses—the rendering of distributions of the sensible—produce understandings of what capacities bodies have and what they can do, as well as set of processes that repress, organize, and communicate haunting matters. In what follows, I illustrate a historical landscape of the images of childhood and childhood art that have bound children into partitions based on preconceived criteria about the capacities of children. Here, it is important to note that I describe *a* historical landscape of childhood studies and childhood art education—rather than *the* history of child art—by focusing on aspects that are considered important to understanding the policing nature of such studies.

A History of Childhood Images

Children and childhood are a constructed matter. To study "the child," therefore, is to look at the cultural, historical, and political context that produces one (Burman, 2017). Childhood images stem from a long history that goes back to as early as Plato's *Republic* where an external person (e.g., the philosopher, educator, or legislator of the *polis*) would give form to another who has no form, who is understood incapable of establishing the form by himself (Plato, 1902). As Platonic "form" is synonymous to "idea,"[2] having no form meant lacking intellectual perception or knowledge about the "truth" of the world, which justified education be necessary for the development of a child for its function of giving a form—to *in*form. In thinking about children regarded as having "no form," it invokes Rancière's (1999) description of those who are unseen and unheard, as having "no part" (p. 30), as the constitutive outside of the distribution of the sensible. Though Rancière has not specifically addressed such thoughts in the context of young children, he has articulated extensively on emancipatory politics and pedagogy on the status of being positioned as a minority, such as the laborer (1989), the poor (2003), the spectator (2007a, 2011), and the student (1991, 2010). As such, bringing Rancièrian perspective to this book, I can only speculate how Rancière might think about the context of early childhood education, and more particularly art education, by alluding to his writings on pedagogy, politics, and aesthetics. Therefore, here, in taking the task of conjecture in what Rancière would attend to within the conflict in the historically, socially, and politically constructed image of childhood (e.g., the deficit model), I again suspect he would argue that childhood images is a part of the distribution of the sensible that has been deeply engraved onto adults' perceptions of children that consequently generated the idea that children lack forms and parts of the society, missing the rights adults have. In fact, what governed the history of child art, as mentioned in the previous chapter, is rooted in a broader notion of childhood, which is again a "matter of constructing a plot" (Rancière, 2016, p. 29). The plot-shaping of childhood is the attempt to organize and impose meanings to childhood by adults' convenience. I view developmental structuralist approaches as an example of constructing a plot in childhood, as they rely on biomedical causation to understand the lives and works of children (e.g., Lowenfeld & Brittan, 1947; Piaget, 1960) that primarily derives from the images of children as lacking social ability. Thus, in order to discuss how such images of childhood have policed children's everyday lives and works, the following illustrates the definition of childhood and the pre-sociological and sociological approaches to understanding childhood.

Child(ren) and Childhood

Because it is difficult to define the child without the conception of the adult and adult society (Jenks, 2005), children are inevitably recognized by their apparent differences, such as biological traits, behaviors, language, and other perceived (in)abilities. In what follows, I unpack the historically, socially, and politically interwoven concept of the child, children, and childhood that adults have theorized and practiced. Though I am critical of adult-centered explanations of childhood, I do not intend to create a dualism between the adult and the child, as it would be a move that further intensifies existing hierarchical social orders, which continue to police children. Therefore, rather than explaining who the child *is*, here I focus on how the child has been *viewed* throughout history. In other words, I attempt to explore the dominant *images* of children in relation to existing philosophical, sociological, and political discourses.

Before I examine the scholarship of childhood studies, I should note that here, I differentiate child(ren) and childhood. While "child(ren)" signifies an individual or a group of people who are not yet adults, the notion of "childhood" is a human condition that is perceived distinctly different from adulthood, that tends to associate with particular images adults have constructed. In fact, I have not yet encountered a child referring to their present status as "childhood." According to James and James (2012), a definition of a *child* is:

> [a] human being in the early stages of its life-course, biologically, psychologically and socially; it is a member of a generation referred to collectively by adults as "children," who together temporarily occupy the social space that is created for them by adults and referred to as "childhood."
>
> (p. 8)

Among the biological and social characteristics of child(ren), *age*, in particular, has been used as a convenient tool to separate children from other social groups, classifying children's physical, psychological, and social development (James & James, 2012). This emphasis on age creates the ultimate "Other," a population is from the onset reliant on the majority population (i.e., adults) for guidance toward maturity and individual independence (Cannella, 1997, p. 19). For example, developmental psychologist Jean Piaget (1960) described children's cognitive and moral development in a deterministic manner, binding children to distinct developmental stages, each designed to represent the child's incremental progression toward adulthood. In this approach, the criterion of age was dominantly employed to define the idea of adulthood and citizenship rather than a genuine impression of the child's intellectual capacities or achievements.

Of course, it is indisputable that the analysis of children's biological development has provided considerable knowledge about the various common changes that young people experience over time. However, using age as the defining marker for this change often engenders restrictions or protections on children's activities (James & James, 2012), which neglects the child's capacity to be in control of their activity. Moreover, the problem rests with this distinction and the separation of time and space as it produces inequalities that bind children—by virtue of being non-adults—to adults' constructions of them, as predetermined human conditions (Foucault, 1975) (see also, e.g.,

MacNaughton, 2005). In other words, the conceptualizations of children have been regulated by adults' power and interests, resulting in the production of oppression and injustice toward children. This is widely and deeply ingrained in adults' perspective, influencing children's everyday lives. As Carla Rinaldi (1998) writes, the image of the child has been "a cultural (and therefore social and political) convention that makes it possible to recognize (or not) certain qualities and potential in children" (p. 116). Attentive to this image and reality of childhood constructed in socio-cultural contexts, the following section maps out the two main threads of childhood: the "pre-sociological" and "sociological" images of the child.

Images of the Child: The "Pre-sociological"

Relativizing the concept of childhood within social contexts, French historian Phillippe Ariès (1965) asserted that childhood has not always been the same thing: in the past, children were viewed as miniature adults expected to behave like grown-ups as soon as possible. However, after the "discovery of children" emerged in the eighteenth century, the view shifted to children being considered as inferior beings in need of adults' strict control. The vision surrounding children is conceived from a series of socio-political discourses, an invention of more contemporary times. Such discourses are informed by the dominant philosophical concepts driven by European models of family and childhood, proposed by white, middle- to upper-class males (e.g., Rousseau, Locke, and Piaget) studying white children in European contexts. In fact, most of the scholars I refer to here, from Rancière to even those who propose critical perspective to childhood studies, are primarily Western scholars and researchers. I would have to ironically refer to Rancière again to unpack this dilemma, as valuing conventional Eurocentric perspective is a "distribution of the sensible" in the majority of scholarships. Yet, because such Eurocentric ideas have widely policed the study of childhood, I find that it is appropriate to describe the historical landscape of how the image of childhood has been constructed, which stretches its influence to the non-Western parts of the world as well.

Herein, I adopt James, Jenks, and Prout's (1998) review of the theoretical models of childhood in *Theorizing Childhood*, from the "pre-sociological" characterization to "sociological," to grasp the conventional perceptions of the child(ren) and childhood. These two distinctly different theoretical views of children shape notions of children's citizenship as either a future status or as a current status. To begin with, the pre-sociological models of childhood are demonstrated as follows: the evil child, the innocent child, the immanent child, the naturally developing child, and the unconscious child. While this list of five major pre-sociological theories is not a definitive way of viewing children, it has informed and continued to inform conceptions about children and their everyday lives from the 1600s to the present. These models were shaped by theories that do not acknowledge the social context and have developed in becoming "part of conventional wisdom surrounding the child" (James et al., 1998, p. 3).

The image of *the evil child* has its foundation in the doctrine of Adamic original sin, regarding children as demonic, subject to potentially dark forces. In the sixteenth century, the child was considered weak and susceptible to evil and therefore needed correct training and discipline to become good citizens. English theologian John Wesley (1703–91), for instance, believed that children are inherently bad and therefore they should be inculcated in order to become good via adults' control and punishment (Heitzenrater, 2001). This image of a child justifies the adults' subjugation of young people to power structures, which corresponds to Michel Foucault's (1975) idea of "docile bodies," bodies that are subject to being used, transformed, and improved.[3] Childhood, in this regard, has its foundation in exercising restraint on the dispositions of corruption, and thus requires discipline and punishment operated by adults.

The most problematic yet most dominant image of childhood is *the innocent child*. This image depicts the child as being in a naïve state, due to their lack of experience or knowledge, and free from moral guilt (James & James, 2012, p. 68). Based on Jean Jacques Rousseau's (1712–78) treatise on children's education described in the book *Emile*, the innocent child is considered inherently good, pure in heart, angelic, and uncorrupted by the world. Also, believing in natural development, education was thus the process of learning about nature, reasons, logic, and objects in the real world. In fact, the eighteenth- and nineteenth-century discourse of the innocent child has become foundational to contemporary child-centered education that considers childhood recognizable through "encouragement, assistance, support, and facilitation" (James et al., 1998, p. 14). Although regarding children as little demons or angels may not be the dominant idea today, theories in early childhood education and adults' everyday engagement with children still gravitate toward one side of the dichotomy, emphasizing either the child's natural development over social demands or what the child must learn to become a good (adult) citizen in the future.

The immanent child is based on John Locke's (1632–1704) ideas that consider children as "no-thing," or in a blank slate, which is fundamentally antithetical to Rancière's (1991) understanding of all people's already-endowed intellectual capacities.[4] This idea that children come to the world as empty pages anticipating to be filled with knowledge given by adults acknowledge children's mental processes and perceptions on a gradient of becoming, moving toward reason. It is believed that all contents of children's mind come from experiences, therefore adults can elicit reasons from children if an appropriate environment is provided. In fact, this model created the general view that children are innately motivated to learn, offering "the earliest manifesto for 'child-centered' education" (Archard, 1993, as cited in James et al., 1998, p. 16), which has its foundation on the belief that education determines everything about a child becoming adult.

In the twentieth century, the image of children became ostensibly more scientific, focusing on their physical, psychological, and emotional development. *The naturally developing child* draws on Swiss psychologist Jean Piaget's (1896–1980) "the stages of cognitive development" (1932, 1960, 1962, 1971) in which children are considered as lacking competence, whereas adults' operative intelligence signifies achieved competence. In this view, children were described as initially egocentric, only capable to develop moral sensibilities and reasoning that comply with expectations for rational thinking only gradually, in a linear progression. Moreover, Piaget's description of children's cognitive and moral development represented the distribution of the sensible, which specific cognitive structures were classified in discrete stages, where an achievement of each being necessary to move into the next stage. As psychology theory dominated the understanding of childhood during this time—namely, behaviorism, measurement and habit formation, and normative child psychology—researchers have constructed specific characteristics as universal truths, of which they believed important to the growth and functioning of the child (Cannella, 1997). The work of Piaget and Inhelder (1969) will be further discussed in the latter part of this chapter, on its relation to visual realism and how it contributed to creating partitions (i.e., stage theories) in childhood art.

The latest pre-sociological image emerged in the late nineteenth and early twentieth century is *the unconscious child*, which is grounded on Sigmund Freud's (1856–1939) understanding that young children are not only sentient and passionate beings but also highly vulnerable to parental and other early influences, affected by the id, ego, and super-ego. In the 1920s, a Freudian context for the interest in children's experience became dominant in public discourse on the child. One of the distinctive features of this discourse is the assumption that unresolved conflicts in childhood persist into adulthood and may become sources for problems later in life. This perspective often yielded exaggerated and distorted understanding of a child, insofar as such ideas only depicted a child as lacking agency and intentionality.

Accordingly, the conception of childhood being established primarily on the basis of developmental psychology has gained epistemological authority and grew prevalent beyond the US context, with its emphasis on sorting and chopping childhood into sections (Galman, 2019). Specifically, the hegemony of developmental psychology, which, in a broader sense materialized from positivism, restricted adults' vision of understanding children only in proportion to developmental stages (Burman, 2017; Tarr, 2003). Since such biomedical conception of the child and seemingly objective scientific methods to analyze children gained international favor in the early twentieth century, the idea that child development is predictable and universal has bound children to the *less-developed* side of the population. For example, the Piagetian understanding of children's development tends to subscribe to the "deficit conception" of childhood, where the nature of the child is viewed primarily as a configuration of deficits, lacking competencies adults possess (Matthews, 2008, 2009). One of the problems of this positivistic view is its tendency to decontextualize children (Kincheloe, 2005; Schulte, 2021), which not only feeds into the assumption that children that children are less-than adults, less-than citizens, less-than artists, or merely a group of bodies not having culture or knowledge, but also minimizes the particularities of the work they produce.

As developmental typologies gained epistemological power, resistance to this growing empire began to arise in the late twentieth century, in which a number of postmodern scholars questioned the underlying universality of these stages for its neglect of the context or the culture that accompanies children's lives (Cannella, 1997; Dahlberg et al., 1999; Walsh, 2005). Gaile Cannella (1997) points out that classifying developmental stages is problematic for their implicit assumptions of a deficit, which consequently marginalizes the child as the "Other" (p. 34). Among the academic discipline, sociology, in particular, arose to challenge the unitary models of child development. Sociologists emphasized the social construction of childhood, a theoretical perspective that explores how the "reality" in different social contexts could depict the idea of childhood differently (Berger & Luckman, 1967). As such, while the pre-sociological models demonstrated series of images, representations, and constructs of a child on the basis of age and maturity, the sociological approach arose with a perspective that acknowledges children's agency with "social, political and economic status as contemporary subjects" (James et al., 1998, p. 26).

The Sociological Approach: The "New" Sociology of Childhood

The awakening of social theory that problematizes the very idea of the child as a pre-stated being within determined trajectories (i.e., developmental stages) has increasingly become a popular perspective in contemporary childhood studies (Qvortrup, 1993). Viewing childhood as a social phenomenon, scholars developed a sociological perspective of which the taken-for-granted realities of everyday life spring from the interactions people engage with one another within the complex milieu, thus moving toward multiple conceptions of childhood (Berger & Luckman, 1967; James & Prout, 1997; Jenks, 2008). Whereas the pre-sociological images of childhood viewed the child as incompetent and vulnerable, the sociological perspective sees the child as competent and autonomous agents, one who is capable of constructing their lives in their own right (e.g., King, 2007; Matthews & Limb, 1998). This shift in paradigm has been called as the "new" sociology of childhood for its focus on children's historical, temporal, and cultural specificity as well as their agency capable of creating meaning through their interactions with adults and peers

(Prout, 2011). Though such views challenge the taken-for-granted notions of childhood, it is not that such a perspective is ignorant of biological characters of humans but rather committed to studying how children become members of the society, as children's socialization is "a process of appropriation, reinvention, and reproduction" in which a communal activity that children "negotiate, share and create culture with adults and each other" (Corsaro, 2015, p. 18).

In viewing the concept of the socially developing child as transitional theorizing of childhood, James et al. (1998) demonstrate four different discourses to childhood from a sociological point of view: *the socially constructed child* perspective that stresses childhood of plurality and diverse constructions; *the tribal child* that intentionality welcomes the anthropological strangeness and such a form of child life; *the minority group child,* which describes a status excluded from complete participation in the social life; and *the social structural child* perspective that views childhood as a social phenomenon and children as body of subjects determined by their society, sharing certain universal characteristics. Whereas the pre-sociological theories perceived children in terms of *becoming* adults, the sociological theories developed in recent decades focus on the "here and now" of children apart from the psychologically deterministic epistemology. These four analytical models do not stand in isolation given that they commonly acknowledge children as competent and capable social actors, as well as the influence of social structures, yet conceptualized in different ways.

Because, paradoxically, a child is socially constructed yet pushed into the margins as a minority in reality, it is important to acknowledge how children's lives are policed in multiple layers and in diverse realms. The sociological viewpoint highlights the particularities of childhood, in lieu of imposing naturalistic and universalistic assumptions. For example, the "socially constructed child" reflects the social, economic, cultural, and historical contexts within which children are embedded, as well as the social structures such as generation, ethnicity, class, and gender in shaping children's lives (Qvortrup et al., 1994), and the "minority group child" attends to the politicization of childhood and the consideration of children as essentially equal to any other age group, as "active subjects" (James et al., 1998, p. 31). Here, the term "minority" is not so much a demographic but moral classification as it primarily considers the "relative powerlessness or victimization" (James et al., 1998, p. 31). This perspective particularly focuses on the structural and ideological issues that assign children to a subordinate status, subject to potentially being positioned as powerless, disadvantaged and oppressed by those with power (i.e., adults) (James & James, 2012; Oakley, 1994). Hence, such deficit discourse has attributed to the marginalized status of children in reality, which is where I find Rancière's description of those who have no parts relevant to the reality of childhood.

The two strands of pre-sociological and sociological—or developmentalism and social constructionism—are not in a distinct binary form but interwoven in a way that produces continuous discussion. Alan Prout (2011) points out that the long neglect of childhood by sociology was due to childhood seemingly "defy[ing] the division between nature and culture" (p. 7). It was the characteristic of childhood that challenged adults' propensity to classify children into the either/or binary. Prout refers to feminist philosopher Donna Haraway (1991), who included childhood—along with madness and women's bodies—to the list of phenomena that eluded modernity. Childhood, like the other phenomena, embraces hybridity: it sits astride the culture or nature binary that the white-male history has constructed, producing unsettlement among those who attempt to fully control and know *about* children. Children being part natural and part social, therefore, suggest that we also stray away from dichotomizing and compartmentalizing them into partitions. Insofar as the history, culture, and society have widely normalized and generalized childhood into categories of "the distribution of the sensible" (Rancière, 2013a), it is essential that we as interested adults attend to childhood by celebrating their hybridity, to allow them to be part of multiple characteristics, in between categories, or to be free from any deterministic definition imposed on them. As such, rather than tidying up these innately heterogeneous characters of the child, children, and childhood, I argue that we attend to the particularities of children's in-betweenness and the subtle yet significant social performances they engage in, which will be further illustrated in Chapters 4 and 5.

The Reality of Childhood

Despite the sociological perspectives of childhood, one area that remains to be contentious is the citizenship of children, one of the ways how the society continues to police and haunt children's everyday experiences. Children, throughout history, have remained in the margins in the discourse of democratic citizenship, being "part of those that have no part" (Rancière, 2015, p. 33) of the distribution of the sensible. They are rarely perceived as actors or participants of the society capable of making claims and demanding rights. Aristotle, who first theorized the notion of citizenship (Faulks, 2000), defined "a citizen" as one who has a rational autonomy capable of governing and to be governed. In describing citizens as political beings, of those with speech, Aristotle (1999) excluded both children and old men for their dependency, along with slaves who lacked the voice to speak. This structure that omits young people as valid citizens maintains until today that characterize children as "not-yet-citizens" (Moosa-Mitha, 2005), "semi-citizens" (Cohen, 2005), "citizens in the making" (Marshall, 1950), or "citizens in waiting" (Cutler & Frost, 2001). It is a view that subscribe to the "less-than" narrative of children, reinforced by the influence of developmental psychology and the images of childhood that regard children as incomplete when compared to the dominant population—the adults. Evoking Rancière's description of the police that distributes what is visible, what can be said, who can speak and act, the idea that who we perceive as citizens is also constructed by a normalized social order. Dobrowolsky (2002) argues that "because the figure of the child is unified, homogeneous, undifferentiated, there is little talk about race, ethnicity, gender, class and disability. Children become a single, essentialized category" (p. 43). The point being is that, just as how adults are given the privilege of consideration that social divisions (e.g., class, race, gender, and disability) affect their citizenship, children's diverse social, cultural, and economic context ought to be equally acknowledged as well.

I must note that legislative endeavors that acknowledge children's agency and political roles in communities *do* exist. Recent international research and policies emphasize its focus on children as citizens, especially after the ratification in 1989 of the United Nations Convention on the Rights of the Child (UNCRC) (Bath & Karlsson, 2016; Cockburn, 2013; James & James,

2012), an international agreement that sets out the civil, political, economic, social, and cultural rights of every child. As Jupp (1990) observes, UNCRC imposes legally binding norms on state parties who ratify the Convention as consensus-building, by which society is held accountable for protecting children's rights. Broader conceptualizations of citizenship that recognize people's lives and socio-cultural background that affect their citizenship have emerged. Isin and Turner (2002) acknowledge that contemporary citizenship theory constructs citizenship not only in terms of legal rights but "as a social process through which individuals and social groups engage in claiming, expanding or losing rights" (p. 4). This understanding of citizenship serves as more hopeful than focusing on the legal definition on citizenship alone, especially thinking about how children might be considered as legitimate citizens for their social, cultural, and material circumstances they embody in everyday lives. Notwithstanding recent efforts to include children as citizens, the everyday language and worlds of children in reality remain very different to those of adults' contemporary public spaces (Corsaro, 2015).

Looking at the images and reality of children, particularly the arrangement that pushes children to perpetual sub-human status, helps us recognize the roots of various behaviors and acts against children as instances of stereotyping childhood and children. The reality is that children are still very much subjected to relentless oppression and micro-aggressions. Issues of child abuse and neglect, child labor, child imprisonment, child pornography, and other behaviors or policies that harm all facets of children's lives and souls remain to exist across the world. Pierce and Allen (1975) demonstrate their concern toward "childism," a term Pierce coined to refer to societal prejudice against children, that it is "the basic form of oppression in our society and underlies all alienation and violence, for it teaches everyone how to be an oppressor and makes them focus on the exercise of raw power rather than on volitional humaneness" (p. 266). In other words, if children continue to be socialized through direct experience of subordination where humanity is segregated between older and younger, racism and sexism inevitably will persist as subsequent acts of discrimination.

In fact, it is no secret that the reality is even more harsh for children of color. Colonial philosopher John Stuart Mill, for example, justified empire and colonialism that "children and savage peoples (who are also considered children) have no inherent rights to bodily integrity or freedom from violence" (Rollo, 2018, p. 313). Today, popular narratives of modern protective innocence are presented as if they reflect the empirically realities of childhood experience. However, because the idea of childhood and innocence is white-European childhood, viewing the child as possessing little moral standing, racialized children are subject to detrimental dehumanization beyond childism prejudices. In the context of the United States, the American white supremacy is reinforced through the exclusive attribution of innocence. Far too often, Black boys in particular are confronted with incidents of antiblackness in their everyday lives, even during play, where they are considered as monstrous and dangerous beings (Bryan & Jett, 2018; Ferguson, 2001; Howard, 2021; Rosen, 2017). In 2014, Tamir Rice, a twelve-year-old African-American boy living in Cleveland, Ohio was killed by a white police officer for carrying a replica toy gun. In 2020, during the Covid-19 pandemic, African-American boy Isaiah Elliot from Colorado was suspended from his school for having a neon green plastic gun visible on the computer screen during a virtual art class and had police visit their home. Black girls, too, are subject to asymmetrical, racialized understanding of innocence. As Bernstein (2011) writes, whereas an imagining of white girls is "tender, innocently doll-like, and deserving of protection," black girls are insensate, "disqualified from all those qualities" (p. 29). The privileges and promises of childhood innocence fail to protect children of color to a great extent, as they do not receive the same kind of empathy afforded to white children. This is an urgent, social reality that we must acknowledge to correct the ill-conceived notions that put young people to structures of degradation. Again, like ghosts, it is the reality and the elusive prejudices that bound children to the partition of less-than beings, thus affecting every mundane activity and engagement with the world.

The History of Childhood Art and Art Education

Ghostly Matters are part of social life. If we want to study social life well, and if in addition we [too] want to contribute, in however small a measure, to changing it, we must learn how to identify hauntings and reckon with ghosts, must learn how to make contact with what is without doubt often painful, difficult, and unsettling.

(Gordon, 1997/2008, p. 23)

Cultural theorist Avery Gordon's (1997/2008) work *Ghostly Matters* builds on Derrida's idea of hauntology to establish a new way of thinking about the exclusions of history. Drawing from C. Wright Mills's (1959) idea that personal experiences are always shaped by broader cultural practices, Gordon uses "ghostly matters" to investigate "that dense site where history and subjectivity make social life" (p. 8). In further investigating the history of childhood art and art education, I adopt Gordon's elaboration on ghostly matters as it aligns with the history that constructed the idea of childhood and how it influences children's personal and social life. As seen in the images and the reality of childhood that persist to haunt children's lives, it is evident that the culturally, historically, and politically constructed notion of childhood forms our everyday understanding of a child and children.

In this part of the chapter, I turn to providing a brief landscape of the history of childhood art. Because the practices children engage in is inseparable from the existing notions of childhood, I find that the idea of child art in the scholarship of art education has shifted in a way that corresponds to James et al.'s (1998) characterization of the pre-sociological and sociological child as well as the prejudices against children. Gordon (1997/2008) comments about "the quiet, unmotivated complicity of those who shut their eyes, go about their daily routines, and find every means available to not know, to shelter themselves from what is happening all around them" (p. 94). Though Gordon states this in relevance to the specific social context of Argentina, this, to me, reads as a wakeup call to what the scholarship of art education might have done to childhood, how we might have silenced the voices and proceeded our daily routines without any intention to know what is happening in children's lives. This, perhaps, suggests a way to confront the ghostly matters in the study and practice of children's art: to be attentive to what we are habitually shutting our eyes on, what we are ignorant of without recognizing, and what the society have trained us to act and exist in certain ways. In what follows, I present accounts of childhood development and how childhood art has been affected by such understandings, particularly on the aesthetics and contents of children's work.

Childhood Art and Developmental Accounts

Despite the recent scholarly endeavors to expand understandings of childhood, developmentalist accounts remain to be the most dominant discourse surrounding childhood and children's artistic practices. As the "developmentalist paradigm" (Burman, 2017) persists, it harvests the idea that childhood art emerges "naturally" in a linear progression and can be associated with concepts of purity or innocence. Among the many criteria scientists have employed to studying a child's artistic development, "age" (James, 2005; James & James, 2012) and the according "competence" (Alderson, 2008a) have been the most ubiquitous measurement. Art education scholar and researcher Christopher Schulte (2021) describes how the instrumental approach of developmental psychology and its criteria have created a concept of "deficit aesthetic," one that distorts children's experience, disempowers the child, and re-affirms the white, Western, middle-class subjectivities. In what follows, I provide a rough landscape of how the deficit model of childhood art became gradually constructed in the field of art education, resulting in affecting the everyday lives and works of children.

As briefly mentioned above, from the nineteenth century psychologists were drawn to the child psychology and development. The study on children's drawing was predominantly in service to other disciplines (i.e., psychology or neuroscience) because it seemingly provided causality for understanding a child's cognitive, linguistic, and intellectual development. This biomedical understanding of children was implemented in many other education-oriented researches during this period of the twentieth century, in which children's art was construed by psychological standards (e.g., Arnheim, 1974; Gardner, 1980; Goodenough, 1926; Kellogg, 1969). A dominant theory in this psychological focus on children's art was the "Mirror paradigm" that examined the ability of the child to represent images of something other than the object itself, which often compared children's drawings to that of *primitive* (Bühler, 1930; Sully, 1896). British psychologist James Sully (1896, 1907), influenced by Freudian and Lacanian psychoanalytic theories, was interested in the self-reflective qualities of children's art that allegedly suggested the inner workings of their minds.

Continuing the work of Sully, psychologists analyzed and classified the development of a child by examining the end product, that of children's drawings: Florence Goodenough (1926) believed a child's intellectual development controlled the nature and content of children's drawings, stating that "the brighter the child, the more closely is his analysis of a figure" (p. 75). Goodenough (1926) introduced the "Draw-a-Man Test" that measured children's cognitive, psychological, and intellectual abilities by using quantitative methods for the assessment of human figure drawings. The test gained popularity among psychologists and other researchers eager to use quantitative scales to measure children's intellectual maturity. The main assessment criterion was the number of details: higher quantitative details manifested in the portrait indicated superiority in intelligence. For example, more numbers of body parts, more details of clothing and accessories, more accurate representation of the facial expressions and gender of the figure, as well as movements of the figure signified superior intelligence (Goodenough, 1926; Harris, 1963/1991).

In the 1930s, Jean Piaget (1932, 1960, 1962, 1971) (see also, Piaget & Inhelder, 1956) presented a developmental theory of organizational and graphic skills based on maturity, which is argued to be connected directed with age. In Piaget's theories, a child's drawing is in the process of assimilation and therefore neither a child's procedural decision makings nor their experience can be a significant factor for understanding the child. The linear understanding of child art development reminds us of the "naturally developing child" image, which every child is believed to develop in predictable stages. To give some credit to this image of childhood, empirical evidence that shows some correlation between the development of the human brain and maturation of the child through chronological age does exist, particularly from the field of brain development, however, this should be understood with the fact that such research has mainly focused on brains of animal, adult human, and children at developmental risks. Any generalization from such models, including the development theory of graphic skills, therefore, are within margins of error.

Viktor Lowenfeld (1947) is widely described as one of the most foundational scholars in twentieth-century art education (Lowenfeld & Michael, 1982). His book *Creative and Mental Growth*, published in 1947 and now in its eighth edition, presented a comprehensive working theory of art expression and human development, particularly classifying children's drawings into six developmental progressions: scribbling, preschematic, schematic, dawning realism, pseudo-naturalistic, and adolescent art. Originating from psychoanalysis, Lowenfeld theorized that, within this linear progression, children's life experiences are integrated into the drawing in an orderly manner, which assumed a certain level of universal predictability and universality in children's drawings. Like Cizek, Lowenfeld believed that adults should not impose their images on a child's art practice, as he found that students lose confidence in their artistic competency because of the seemingly toxic adult influences. This stage theory of Lowenfeld continues to be the most widely used typology of children's graphic development in the field of art education (Schulte, 2021). It is important to note that I do not intend to discredit Lowenfeld's contribution to the scholarship of art education, as his work has been indeed monumental in the United States and Western art education, more broadly. Yet I do wish to carefully point out that the act of compartmentalizing children's art contributes to the dominant idea that childhood development is predictable and universal therefore adults hold the power to deduct epistemological conclusions about children. Moreover, this is what Rancière would see as police, constructing partitions of the sensible that leaves little room to think or do outside of the given assignments. Namely, Schulte (2021) points out that "within Lowenfeld's typology, younger children will always be positioned as less competent and less skilled than older children, and especially so in relation to adults" (p. 61).

Following Lowenfeld's stages, a myriad of theories and numerical analysis of child art sprung on the basis of developmental typologies continued to dominate the field until late twentieth century (see Arnheim, 1974; Gardner, 1980; Kellogg, 1969; Kindler & Darras, 1997; Lark-Horovitz et al., 1967) yet persists in somewhat recent studies as well (e.g., Kouvou, 2016). The classification of child art based on psychological standards remains to be controversial as it neglected the particularities and vicissitudes of children in many aspects, especially where "the equation of details with intelligence [being] far too simple to be reliable" (Duncum, 2018, p. 225). For example, Goodenough's (1926) "Draw-a-man-test" intentionally eliminated any sociological aspect of a child, such as language, verbal skills, emotion, or collaboration with others, implies that adults' ultimate interest rested on controlling knowledge *about* children, mainly about their development. In other words, rather than seeing children as social agents, it was only their end products that were indicative of something worth to study.[5]

Art education scholars Brent and Marjorie Wilson (1981) critiqued the studies on developmental stages by proposing three reasons: developmental approaches to children's drawings were primarily conducted decades ago in Western culture (e.g., the United States and Europe); assume a natural, spontaneous innate unfolding as an unfettered and uninfluenced process that consequently lack searching for any other explanations; and fail to deal with themes, of which the variety of ways in which children compose pictures, as well as gender-related differences (pp. 4–5). The theorization based on developmental stages, to put it into Rancièrian terms, merely resulted in a "distribution of the sensible" that assigned children's art into particular places susceptible to the hierarchical orders. It polices the perception of children's art to discern what is visible or noticeable in their work while other aspects are not as important to pay attention to.

In the late twentieth century, scholars who believed that there are alternative approaches to developmentalist normalization of child art emerged. Such idea has been continued and supported by literature in the field of art education today, highlighting the contextualized, complex matters of children's lives and works (Ivaskevich, 2009; McClure, 2013; Park, 2019; Park & Schulte, 2021; Pearson, 2001; Sakr, 2017; Sakr & Osgood, 2019; Schulte, 2011, 2015a, 2015b, 2018; Sunday, 2015, 2018; Thompson & Bales, 1991; Thompson, 1995, 2002, 2009; Wilson & Wilson, 1982; Wilson & Wilson, 1984, Wilson, 2005, 2008a, 2008b). Focusing on the pluralities and particularities in children's art practices, such works have highlighted the generational characteristics of children, such as visual culture and popular culture influences (e.g., McClure, 2007; Shin, 2016; Thompson, 2003, 2006; Wilson, 2005, 2007) and the use of digital methods in art practices (e.g., Ivashkevich & shoppell, 2013; Knight, 2018; Sakr, 2017, 2019), along with gender-related understandings (e.g., Bae-Dimitriadis, 2015; Ivashkevich, 2009; McClure, 2006) and various other socio-culturally influenced aspects.

Though my thoughts on compartmentalizing children's works on the basis of age and maturity align with critiques to developmentalistic arrangements, it is not to demonize the psychologists' and art education scholars' attempts of studying child art. In fact, such attempts originate from good intention and inquiry on yearning to know about children and their works. However, what I do find problematic is that such classification on children's art maintains as an invisible yet ubiquitously controlling force in education, despite today's disciplinary climate that does not explicitly advocate the theorization of children's art based on age and maturity. It is the presumption that adults, and even children themselves, internalize the idea that a certain age is expected to draw and make art in particular ways and forms, which continues in the realm of the style and contents of children's art, or in other words, how and what children draw.

Aesthetics and Contents of Childhood Art

In the manner of how adults have partitioned children's art based on age, developmental capacities, and other biomedical standards, the content of children's art—what they draw *about*—and the resulting style have been significantly policed as well, as a particular kind of a distribution of the sensible. Namely, adults often present approval and interest when children draw about general life events (e.g., birthday parties, nature, school life, family, animals, etc.), whereas seemingly age-inappropriate contents and aesthetics (e.g., violence, eroticism, and etc.) tend to raise concerns and ultimately censored by adults, and even peers. This, too, exists as a normalized framework in art education settings, policing everyday art practices of children. Considering how adults' perceptions on what is proper content or aesthetic[6] in children's drawing and what is not persist to haunt the children and the field of art education today, I illustrate here how such notions gained timeless power throughout the historical shifts in art education.

The police on children's graphic development on the basis of age and maturity has consequently policed particular modes of child art throughout the history. The idea that children's artworks even have a sense of aesthetic is, in fact, a relatively new one. Children's drawings have been either "ignored, found amusing, or ridiculed" until the nineteenth century, which is when modernism allowed the appreciation of "inventive, primal and authentically expressive modes of work that adults became able to value the art of children for its own special aesthetic qualities" (Leeds, 1989, pp. 95–96). It is when the fashions of adults' aesthetics changed upon the introduction of new forms and movements of art (e.g., Avant-garde) that subsequently affected the aesthetic standards of child art. The terminology "child art," in fact, was not recognized until Franz Cizek discovered it and named it in the early 1900s (Viola, 1936). Schooling in Austria of late nineteenth and early twentieth century was approached rigidly under harsh disciplines (Michael & Morris,

1985). As briefly mentioned in the previous chapter, in school art classes, drawing was taught in schools by giving children pages of dots: children were asked to connect the dots with straight lines, and, as the age advanced, only the gap between the dots were further apart (Viola, 1936). Valuing seemingly intuitive renderings in children's artworks, one of Cizek's beliefs was that adult influences were detrimental to the "natural" creation of children, and therefore any intervention from the adult world would contaminate the child's original drawing. In other words, the "child-like" characteristics in children's works (e.g., spontaneity and the use of vivid colors in early childhood art) that were treasured by the adults constituted the image of what child art looked like.

Accordingly, the study and teaching practice in art education valued child-like elements in the artworks produced by children. In early twentieth century, Franz Cizek taught children child-like characteristics in his studio and psychologists chopped the works of children into partitions. Cizek's belief in the "original" creation of children and his criticism on any adult influence in children's art practice reflects the "innocent child" image. Similar to Rousseau's treatise of children as pure and uncorrupted by the world, Cizek treasured the naturally occurring artworks of children and taught "decorative and sentimental child art style" (Duncum, 1982, p. 34). Resembling how Cizek instructed his students in the 1920s by assigning particular subjects, materials, rules, aesthetics, and presentation of art to all the students in his class (Greenberg, 1996; Leeds, 1989; Viola, 1936; Wilson, 2004, 2007), art teachers at schools selected topics of art *for* children attending to more of the adult's interest and standards. That is, the style of "school art" (Efland, 1976) was created, controlling the aesthetics of child art to render "the appearance of creativity" (Wilson, 2004, p. 277). As school art is often in service to other school subjects or recreative functions rather than being a legitimate independent subject, the style children were encouraged to adhere to in their artwork was controlled by the adults, ostensibly resembling a child's creative or imaginative capacities. His practice of appropriating ready-made aesthetics implies that child art has been regarded as mere objects—a controllable "thing" distinctive from that of adults.

Moreover, how children draw is intricately interwoven to *what* they draw. The "what" in child art is recognized by adults' set of preconceived knowledges and images, as incomprehensible renderings (e.g., scribbles or unidentifiable figures to the adults' eyes) are often dismissed as "unimportant." However, even within the visually identifiable contents, adults often police whether it is appropriate for a child to draw. One example is the reception of popular cultural images in children's art. Often times at school classrooms, popular culture is reserved for "playtimes" or informal spaces, rather than a resource for formal activities (Yoon, 2018). This is because media-inspired contents in children's writing or drawing activities could be "ideologically unsettling" (Dyson, 1997, p. 3) for adults, since the stories and images are subject to insinuating sexist or racist stereotypes and physical aggression. Thus, these concerns result in establishing classroom rules, for example, restricting the times and occasions stories and images of media culture could appear in teacher-led activities.[7]

The field of art education, too, has been keen to popular cultural influences in children's art practices (Duncum, 1987, 2009, 2014; Ivashkevich, 2009; McClure, 2013; Thompson, 2003, 2006, 2017; Wilson, 1974, 1997; Wilson & Wilson, 1984). Wilson (2007) acknowledges that children's self-initiated works that contain visual cultural contents were unnoticed and regarded as unimportant by adults during the twentieth century, mainly because children created such drawings in their leisure time on their own. Today, amalgamated with the advent of social media that allows a more accessible visual cultural platform for children and youth, it is now virtually impossible to avoid the presence of popular-culture-inspired images and stories in the works of children (Bae-Dimitriadis, 2015; Castro, 2012; Castro et al., 2016; Shin, 2016).

When it comes to the debate of incorporating popular culture into art education curriculum, it reveals the recurring phantom that yearns for the control over what children can or cannot appreciate, consume, and produce in their art practices. In reviewing the hauntological shifts in the field of art education, art education scholar Kevin Tavin (2005) focuses on visual culture that emerged in early 2000s in service to legitimatize the discipline of art education. Also referring to Derrida's elaboration on hauntology, Tavin argues that ideological stratifications on popular culture have continued to haunt art education by disparaging the mass-produced images' influence in children's art (e.g., comic books, films, and TV shows) thus police art education curricula in schools to persist the view that they are the opposite of high culture (Eisner, 1978), as Kitsch or a disregard toward aesthetic contemplation (Efland, 2004). Though neither consensually regarded as explicitly detrimental nor educationally conducive, popular culture consumption and production in educational settings maintain as a contentious matter to *adults*. In other words, the possibility of a disapproval toward children's shared culture itself exemplifies adults' potential control on what children can consume or produce and what they cannot, using their power that could possibility to force their decisions on them. Overall, it is important to note that the example of popular culture is only a fragment of many other occasions where adults' beliefs police the content and style of children's art practices.

This review on the study and teaching of childhood art is far from exhaustive. My focus on the various policing accounts existent in the study of childhood art is rather to point to a type of distribution of the sensible that demands our attention to think differently, toward a nonlinear, contextualized understanding of childhood art. Continuing this discussion, the last chapter of this book illustrates how emancipatory perspectives of childhood art could be imagined, while recognizing the fact that such police will always remain beyond the progression of time, as Rancière (1991) puts it as "inevitable."

An Aesthetico-Ethnographic Inquiry

Event #1. As I am sitting with the girls at the art table, Sophie asks me to draw a picture of Moana. Having watched the Disney film *Moana* about five months ago, I proudly declare that I had watched the movie and therefore would be able to draw Moana without looking up the image on my phone. As I proceed to draw, Sophie makes another request: "Can you draw a picture of Maui after?" I ask, "Maui?" Sophie quickly responds, "Yes." I'm puzzled, because what she just said did sound like the name of Hawaiian island Maui, which was still contextually relevant, however unusual for Sophie, who had been making drawing requests of princesses and popular culture figures, to ask me to draw a shape of an island. In doubt, I ask, "Uh … just the shape of the island?" Sophie then slowly pronounces the word for me, "No, Mau-ee." Still confused, I foolishly say, "So … Moana?" Sophie repeats, "No, Mau-ee." I realized that, clearly, it was not something I knew about. "Okay, so what does Maui look like?" I asked. Katie, who was drawing next to me, nonchalantly urges, "Find a picture on your phone." Sophie begins to describe it for me: "So Maui looks like … " And then, Zoey, sitting next to Sophie, adds, "Also has curly hair like Moana." Despite these descriptions, I still had no apprehension of the figure, or if it *was* even a human figure. I eventually grabbed my phone and typed in "Moana Mawee" at the Google search window. Google's auto-correct function directed me to showing the images of Maui, one of the main characters in the movie Moana, at which point I felt completely stranger to children's popular culture, a realization that showed my earlier feeling of confidence to be misguided.

Field notes, January 30, 2018

As I delve into the research of children's art, my orientation aligns more with exploration of rather than the discovery of an absolute truth. In fact, the nature of society does not contain or clearly demonstrate an absolute truth that could be understood in an explanatory fashion, though the presentation and reproduction of social orders in the study of childhood, historically, has run parallel to the logic of explication. Namely, the commonsense hierarchy that is made to exist between the adult and child, and that is reiterated through adults' attempts of explication of children that fails to value and contextualize their voices and intellectual capacities. For instance, the dominant idea in education represents that a master explicator is needed when a child's own will is not yet strong enough to independently speak, act, and think. This posits children within spaces that make them subjects to stultification (i.e., as having "no part") and merely produces inequality in educational settings and more broadly in any dichotomously constructed child-adult relationships. Attuned to the politics and aesthetics discussed earlier, I take an antithetical position and argue that children are also capable of participating in aesthetico-political experiences. To further illustrate my approach to studying children's art, this chapter first discusses my research methodology, which I term an "aesthetico-ethnographic case study." Then, a call for a more democratic methodology in the future is suggested, that we stay open-minded toward different and new methodological approaches to the study of children.

Ethnographic Practices in Childhood Studies

Before I present my rather unconventional implementation of ethnographic methods, I find it essential to present what conventional ethnography is and looks like, as my aesthetico-ethnographic case study is heavily grounded on the traditional methods in ethnography and childhood anthropology, more broadly. The term "ethnography" represents both process and product of a study. Derived from "ethno," people, nation, or culture, and "graphy," the writing about or study of, "ethnography" is a method designed to study cultures or cultural phenomena. Wolcott (1999) defines ethnography in the following way:

The underlying purpose of ethnographic research ... is to describe what the people in some particular place or status ordinarily do, and the meanings they ascribe to what they do, under ordinary or particular circumstances, presenting that description in a manner that draws attention to regularities that implicate cultural process.

(p. 68)

To paraphrase, ethnography is a descriptive study of a particular human culture that the ethnographer seeks to know about by being immersed into the everyday lives of the cultural community. Rather than imposing outsider knowledge, it is observing and participating in the natural occurrences of a cultural group.

Traditionally, anthropologists employed ethnographic methods, most commonly as participant-observation (e.g., Fine & Glassner, 1979), to understand the culture of the "exotic" (e.g., Malinowski, 1929; Mead, 1928), in which the particular cultural group is observed, documented, written about, and interpreted. In the fieldwork of the study, ethnographers position themselves as a simultaneous participant-observer of the cultural or social group/system, interacting with and/or participating in the day-to-day lives of those they study for a prolonged period (Creswell & Poth, 2018). The process of ethnographic fieldwork includes methods such as jotting down field notes (see Emerson et al., 2011), taking visual documentations (e.g., photo or video) that could later materialize into "narrative" forms (Richardson & St. Pierre, 2005), and/or one-on-one interviews with members of the group for discerning patterns and cultural behaviors in human social activity, as the goal of research is to comprehend the particularities of the cultural group. The product of ethnography refers to the ways in which these cultural behaviors are interpreted and the particular textual form that they are translated into. Based on the collection of notes and documentations, ethnographers portray what was seen and experienced as vividly as possible by providing a "thick description" (Geertz, 1973) and by doing so they *contextualizes* the particular culture through their perspective. This, I believe, is what exists at the core of writing ethnographies, as it could only be materialized by the researcher's immersion in the culture being affected by their positionality and membership roles in the community.

In the context of childhood research, ethnography has become the "new orthodoxy" (James, 2001, p. 246; see also Qvortrup, 2000), as it incorporates children's "direct voice and participation in the production of sociological data, as opposed to other scientifically experimental or survey styles of research" (James & Prout, 1997, p. 8). The beginnings of childhood ethnography were rooted in the discipline of anthropology. Early anthropologists critical to developmental formulations found in psychology, and who pioneered the "anthropology of childhood" (Benedict, 1934, 1955; Boas, 1974; Fortes, 1949; Malinowski, 1929; Mead, 1928), used the interpretive tradition of ethnography to study the cultural variation of children's lives and practices. In studying the ways children acquire and construct culture, the ethnographic field work of these studies was conducted in diverse parts of the world, reflecting a diversity of ethnographic data, that entailed for example, a focus on kinship, religion, family, life cycle, psychological development, and other topics relating to children's lives (Levine, 2007). Modern scholars and educators have increasingly come to view children as active constructors of their own culture, research focusing on the cultural particularities and children's experiences have been expanded in recent decades (e.g., Balagopalan, 2014; Cook-Gumperz et al., 1986; Corsaro, 1985, 2003; Dyson, 2003; Ferguson, 2001; Thorne, 1993).

Children's culture, as all cultures do, contains a shared understanding of beliefs, activities, routines, artifacts, values, knowledge, and concerns (Corsaro & Eder, 1990). In using ethnographic methods to explore children's culture, researchers often embody the "tribes of childhood" (James et al., 1998) orientation, viewing children's culture as "an independent place with its own folklore, rituals, rules and normative constraints ... within a system that is unfamiliar to [adults] and therefore to be revealed through research" (p. 29). This approach allows the ethnographer to de-familiarize certain notions about children and childhood but instead regard them as the anthropologically strange, in order to construe varying details of the culture through new perspectives. Although primarily shared with child peers, children's culture is in fact in close relation with the adult world. Corsaro and Eder (1990) point out:

Children creatively appropriate information from the adult world to produce their own unique peer cultures. Such appropriation is creative in that it both extends or elaborates peer culture (transforms information from the adult world to meet the concerns of the peer world) and simultaneously contributes to the reproduction of the adult culture.

(p. 200)

In other words, children reenact the observed imagery of adults' social rites and events in their activities (e.g., in imaginative play), thus produce and consume particular cultural forms that reside in both the adults' world and the child's. As such, rather than living in a distinct partition of the adult-child binary, "children are always participating in and are part of two cultures—children's and adults'—and these cultures are intricately interwoven" (Corsaro, 2015, p. 26). By simultaneously participating in both worlds, children acquire the conventions of communication relevant to their local and social community, and also "use and modify them for their own purpose" (LeVine & New, 2008, p. 3).

Similar to the children's minority status in society, young people's marginalization also prevails in the practice of research. Despite the preponderance of child(ren) and childhood research in diverse disciplines, researchers often inflict adult-centric biases on the study of children, treating them "as if they are malleable or as if their worlds are timeless and ideal" (Knupfer, 1996, p. 139). This propensity merely reproduces the romanticized images of childhood (e.g., the innocent and immanent child) thus reiterates inequalities children are already faced with in their everyday lives. If such approaches aimed to research *about* children from the adults' point of view, recent studies have devised methods to research *with* children by actively involving children as co-researchers, arguing for children to be regarded as valid participants in research (Alderson, 2008b; Clark, 2003; Clark & Moss, 2001; Kellet, 2006).

Upon the inception of childhood studies, a commitment to child-focused research has been one of the priorities and researchers have developed techniques to that enabled children's perspectives and voices to be incorporated in the research, and moreover, some researchers have explored the ways in which children themselves could take the role as a researcher (James & James,

2012). For example, some studies had the research projects designed by children as co-authors (Kellet, 2006) or photographs taken by the children involved in the research as data (e.g., Clark, 2003; Kondo & Sjöberg, 2012; Templeton, 2021; Vellanki & Davesar, 2020). Authoring direct participation to children also engendered resistance, due to certain methodological, contextual, and/ or ethical issues, such as responsibility, payment, or safety concerns (James & James, 2012). Anthropologist Lawrence Hirschfeld (2002) argues that the resistance to child-focused research in anthropology could be a result of "an impoverished view of cultural learning that overestimates the role adults play and underestimates the contribution that children make" (p. 611). It is another realm where the deficit image of children prevails, grounded on the criteria of age and maturity, even when the study is about children. In other words, while children's adept skills to acquire adult culture were acknowledged, their less obvious ability to create their own culture has been undervalued, resulting in the marginalization of child-focused research (Hirschfeld, 2002). While children have been considered passive recipients of culture—a culture that is primarily conceptualized and consumed by adults—they have not been viewed as active participants or producers of a culture that is understood to be their own.

Yet, a researcher can highlight the equally capable agency of children by assuming a sense of equality between the adult and the child. Namely, equality could be attained by subverting the presumption that certain people *have a part* while others neither can have a part nor the ability to speak, which is what Rancière (1991) described as the binary between intelligences. Instead of subscribing to this dominant binary, intellectual equality commences when it is postulated as a belief from the beginning rather than a result to be achieved at the end. Importantly, this concept of equality in childhood research is more of an ethical orientation than a methodological approach. Though ethics invites a broader spectrum of disciplines, it is not to insinuate an "easier" implementation. Embracing equality between children and adults below the surface of what is ostensibly set forth as methods produces a much difficult decision makings and continuous reflection and negotiation within the self, as well as with others.

The Distribution of the Sensible in Childhood Research

Inasmuch as the distribution of the sensible is immanent in any social parts, it most certainly functions in the realm of research, whereby knowledge is produced, distributed, and consumed via particular institutionalized conceptions that determine "who possesses speech and who merely possesses voice" (Rancière, 2004b, p. 24). Rancière, in fact, demonstrates antithetical views toward the discourses of sociology and social history, and even questions the epistemology such analysis takes for granted (Genel, 2016, p. 13). This is not because of the quality of the methodology of data collection or analysis, but rather because of "the presuppositions made in reading data, or more specifically, with the way a discipline positions its own discourse with respect to that of the object of study" (Pelletier, 2009, p. 272). Methodology, in this sense, is also subject to the modes of distributions, for its innate use of depicting the social world in a particular form and logic. Put differently, what gets to be named as "methodology," connotes that an implicit law and logic exist in the realm of research that determines the inclusion and exclusion of certain approaches. Cultural theorist Caroline Pelletier (2009) writes:

> Disciplinary discourse therefore functions as a distribution of positions, and as the demonstration of the truth of this distribution. This means that the construction of the object of study is not primarily methodological—in the sense of methodology as epistemological starting point or as procedure of verification.
>
> (pp. 272–273)

In the case of qualitative research methodologies, what could be named as ethnography, grounded theory, or phenomenological approach, implies that there are proper forms and models of methods to be categorized as such methodology. In other words, methodologies and disciplinary discourses often function in *mimesis*, like the representational regime of art, subject to habitual approaches to the doing of research and knowledge production. What happens, then, to the studies that reside in in-between methodologies that suspend the policing of the distribution of the sensible in research that governs the definition of a fixated name of methodology? How might an ethnographic practice re-distribute the sensible of research? More particularly, how might researching with child participants disrupt the distribution of sensible through a heterogeneous methodology, one that presumes and verifies equality? As I linger on these inquiries through Rancièrian thoughts, I have reached to an inclination to explore how attending to a research methodology could constitute a sense of *aesthetics* by dissociating with the preexisting distribution of the sensible, the predominant frameworks that prevail as given. Focusing on the point that the struggle for equality[1] is political and therefore aesthetic, the following section explores the emergence and production of aesthetics in ethnographic practices.

The Aesthetics of Ethnographic Practice

Building on the legacy of ethnography in childhood research, I contend that ethnography has an innate aesthetic dimension, both in the process and in the product that it generates. Consistent with the concept of Rancièrian aesthetics mentioned in previous chapters, aesthetics, here, is "a historically determined concept … which is inscribed in a reconfiguration of the categories of sensible experience and its interpretation" (Rancière, 2006b, p. 1). This is also consonant with Rancière's (2011, 2013a, 2015) conceptualization of art, specifically "the aesthetic regime of art," a notion of properly speaking a particular regime for purposes of identifying and thinking about the arts. The aesthetic regime of art, according to Rancière, comes after the representational regime of art, in which art is subsumed under the hierarchy of social and political occupations: the genres serving the dignity of their subject matter, and the primacy of the art of speaking in actuality (Rancière, 2013a).

In thinking about this definition of aesthetics in relation to research methodologies, or more importantly, the *practice* of research, I see it as a re-distribution of the sensible, which determines a mode of articulation in-between forms of action, production, perception, and thought in knowledge production. That is, like Jacotot and his students' pedagogical experience liberated them from being bound to the usual roles that society had assigned to them, an aesthetic experience entails "a change in the regime of belief, the change of the rapport between what the arms know how to do and what the eyes are capable of seeing" (Rancière, 2006b, p. 4). Namely, it is a political enactment that disrupts common sense, the familiar logic of bodies' doing, seeing, and thinking in particular ways, which, in the case of research, might involve certain roles and actions that the researcher or participants engage in. Disruption, as I use in this book consistently as a good thing, is not the end of its story but always serves a greater sense of relation; the break and relations are inextricably bound. The disruption of conventional methods of research, too, produces new ways of doing research and allows us to imagine an aesthetic dimension to emerge.

Unfolding the aesthetic dimension in research methodologies and practice reminds me of performance theorist and ethnographer Phillip Vannini's (2015) elaboration of "non-representational research," a research approach that strays away from the identities of representational methods (e.g., repetition, structures, and/or resemblance), but rather seeks experimental, novel, and even temporal knowledge in doing research. Vannini (2015) writes how to do nonrepresentational research by conceptualizing five imperative attributes: (1) *events* that invite the possibilities of future, rather than pre-established plans, suggesting creative engagements; (2) *relations* that highlight the associations human engage with, including human and nonhuman materials; (3) the *doings*, as performance, in essence, is the possibility of practice and taking things into action; (4) *affective resonances* as the body's capacity, to move and affect other people and other things; and (5) the *backgrounds*, or the atmosphere, that creates possibilities of events, practice, performance, and affects (pp. 7–9). In Rancièrian language, nonrepresentational methodology entails a dissensus from representational research that often demands producing the knowledge of sameness, serving the explicatory purpose of a study policed by preconceived notions or conclusions. This divergence from representation is what I believe makes research "aesthetic," the search for something different, something new, and something contextually particular that affects the researcher and the participants' practice, or doings, in willingly dissociating with the lines of expected structure in research.

In light of this, I argue that ethnography constitutes aesthetics both in process and in the products that it produces: first, the process of fieldwork that rejects discovering a one-right "truth," and second, the writing that encapsulates the process of disrupting the often hierarchical role of the researcher and participants. First, the process of ethnographic method unfolds its aesthetic dimension when it veers away from searching for the one-right-truth. A qualitative ethnographic method is unlikely to conclude with a fixated fact or a clear result. Rather, the nature of ethnography allows the researcher to encounter emergent knowledges and cultural experiences by being immersed in the culture of the group, which might yield a discursive conclusion that is mainly story-telling and question-raising. Instead of going after an absolute truth in order to resolve the research question—a reality that serves an explanatory order of resolving the research problem set forth—the aesthetic fieldwork of ethnography, however, demands that the ethnographer produce multiple interpretations. The ethnographer's presence is contingent on the relations shared with participants, and the ethnographic practice of listening to, participating in, and interacting with a cultural community culminates in a multifaceted understanding of the culture and people. In doing so, an ethnographic practice provokes diverse, contextually situated interpretations of a culture rather than a single-answer conclusion. Again, this is not a new idea but an approach that ethnographers traditionally have been embodying when going into the field. My intention is to highlight this as an aesthetic endeavor, to provide a different perspective through Rancière's theories.

Identifying himself as a storyteller or a polemicist, Rancière posits an agnostic standpoint toward the idea of "truth," as it entails linear modes of explication and representation. His perspective on today's common intellectual discourses that search for the one-right answer is that they are "discourses that usually aim to *get at* truth rather than to proceed *in spite of* truth" (Bingham & Biesta, 2010, p. 132, original emphasis). Here, the notion of truth closely aligns with the myth of explanatory education described in *The Ignorant Schoolmaster*, which compels one to talk about the truth that is agreed upon. It implies that something exists out there as an absolute fact, performing as a force to reach a valid conclusion and often limit possible methods to arrive at a conclusion. However, setting an assumption that there could be multiple understandings, even when a dominant "truth" seems to exist, emancipates one from factual thinking and allows the focus to be concentrated on the particularities of an event. Emancipation, to Rancière, is not simply about moving from a minority group to a majority group, but rather denotes a "rupture in the order of thing" (Rancière, 2003, p. 219). In other words, it disrupts the configuration of the oppositional relationship of one who dominates and one who is subjected to domination. This suggests that, though some early anthropologists have had undertaken approaches to *get at* truths about "Others," an ethnographic practice encourages the ethnographer to focus on the participants' narratives as a cultural storyteller *in spite of* predominant notions of reality, which makes possible the ethnographic practice to be aesthetic.

I continue this thought within the discourse of childhood studies. Attitudes toward definitive knowledges about children have prevailed throughout history and remain, even today, as fact. For example, psychologically informed theories of child development continue to be regarded as *the* standard for how we think about and approach the complex and diverse experiences of children and childhood. By virtue of the distinct differences between adults and children, it has often been the case that research concerning childhood resided in an explanatory method that stultifies children rather than an approach that emancipates them from predominant ideas of childhood. To further illustrate this point, in some early ethnographic literature, wide cultural variations in childhood environments were evinced by anthropologists' generalization about childhood (e.g., DuBois, 1944; van Gennep, 1960; Weisner & Gallimore, 1977), which demonstrated that people divergently agreed upon a universal concept of what constitutes normal child psychological and social development. As the works strove to achieve knowledges and truths *about* children, viewing them as research subjects, the diversified milieu of children's experiences and its particularities were overlooked. In fact, studying the heterogeneity of childhood demands one embody the approach of researching *with* children, on the basis of an equal standpoint. When researchers take the position of researching about children, it often entails a desire to *get at* truth, whereas researching *with* children embraces a move to proceed *in spite of* truth (Bingham & Biesta, 2010). In other words, the former accompanies a sense of equality of which both the researcher and children contribute to the inquiry by activating each intellectual capacity, while the latter prioritizes the researcher's own determination to discover a type of knowledge associated with children. For example, in the opening vignette of my drawing with kindergarten children, it ostensibly illustrates my ignorance to popular culture. However, it could be seen that I proceeded to draw *in spite of* the truth that the gap of cultural knowledge existed (e.g., the apparent gap between what I think of Maui and children's expertise on it), and thereby actively incorporated the child's voices to research *with* them, receptive to emergent events that constitute diverse ideas of children's lives.

The second point I propose is that an aesthetic dimension unfolds in the product of ethnography via challenging the dichotomy of the researcher (the adult researcher) and the research subject (children), which is on the basis of this same challenge in the process of ethnographic fieldwork. As ethnography is the idea of "textualization" (Clifford & Marcus, 1986; Emerson et al., 2011), a researcher's positionality, perspectives, and the relationships built with participants work toward being translated into texts. This procedure of translation manifests through the researcher's own lens, comprises lived experiences and worldviews. Namely, it is "the peculiar practice of representing the social reality of theirs through the analysis of one's own experience in the world of these others" (Maanen, 2011, p. xiii). In studying the world of Others, early anthropologists have often objectified the people they study, regarding them as research "subjects." This orientation directs the researcher to exert a degree of superiority over the participants in both fieldwork and writing, viewing them as mere objects who do not—and often cannot—know. As seen in *The Ignorant Schoolmaster*, Rancière is antithetic to this act of stultification that renders an intellectual binary among people. As this notion of equality is not limited to pedagogy, writing could be a specific distribution of the sensible that suspends the representational modes of speech. Rancière argues:

> Writing, as I understand it, rests on the presupposition of equality. To write means to consider that anyone and everyone is the legitimate addressee of your discourse and, at the same time, that yours is the discourse of a researcher addressing his peers.
>
> (Rancière, 2017, pp. 195–196)

Opposed to the act of stultification that merely perpetuates intellectual divisions, Rancière assumes equality as a presupposition to be set forth when writing about others and therefore undermines the ostensibly legitimate order of discourse that society formulated in consensus. This type of writing, in fact, shifts the distribution of the sensible, providing a platform for people whose voices are not heard in the world, to speak and make their lives visible. In other words, it is an act of dissensus, as dissensus is not so much an institutional overturning but rather "an activity that cuts across forms of cultural and identity belonging and hierarchies between discourses and genres, working to introduce new subjects and heterogeneous objects into the field of perception" (Corcoran, 2015, p. 2). As one of the main modes in the work of perception, writing functions as a powerful act of dissensus, a practice of equality.

The notion of taking any individual(s) seriously as legitimate research participants is especially vital in the case of research with and about children, given that children have been continuously pushed to the margins of research rather than being considered as legitimate addressees. As such, amplifying children's already endowed voices should be a central purpose of research, one that sets out to establish equality between the adult writer/researcher and child participants. An example of this approach to intellectual equality in writing about others could be found in Rancière's own historical writing of French workers' movements in nineteenth century: *The Nights of Labor* (1989). While, at that time, others read the texts of the workers as documents about their labor conditions, he read them as literary and philosophical texts, to challenge the boundary that separates genres. Rendering close relationship between subject and method, Rancière describes:

> *La nuit des prolétaires* was a "political" book in that it ignored the division between "scientific" and "literary" or between "social" and "ideological," in order to take into account the struggle by which the proletariat sought to reappropriate for themselves a common language that had been appropriated by others, and to affirm transgressively the assumption of equality.
>
> (Rancière, in Guénoun & Kavanagh, 2000, p. 5)

The workers who were invisible and had no place by the distribution of the sensible were taken as sensible artists capable of producing literary works in Rancière's perception and his textualization about them. In this sense, returning to childhood ethnographies, when the textualization of children's culture firmly situates children as sensible, knowledgeable participants equal to any other cultural members and knowledge producers, it unfolds an aesthetic dimension where both the researcher and children benefit from the democratic relationships.

As the writing of ethnography is what the diverse processes of fieldwork materialize into as a product. When equality is situated from the starting point between the researcher and participants, it leverages the writing of ethnography to be in the domain of equality. By equality, again, I do not mean a utopian idea of equalness between the adult and the child, but the "intellectual equality" Rancière (1991) suggests through the story of Jacotot, where the master and the students presumed that both parts could equally contribute to the learning experience by actively acknowledging ignorance and activating the "relationship of will to will" (p. 13). For instance, my exchange with the kindergarten children in drawing Maui shares some resemblance with Jacotot's experience with his students, as the children demonstrated their shared cultural knowledge, and I activated the presupposition of considering them as legitimate research participants. Despite the disparity between popular cultural knowledge and language, the children and I eventually worked toward producing a drawing with the help of Internet—similar to Jacotot's use of a bilingual edition of *Télémaque,* or "the minimal link of a thing in common" (Rancière, 1991, p. 2)—which I then textualize the experience here in this book. In fact, this notion of promoting equality through the form of writing is not foreign to the scholarship of childhood studies, as educators and researchers have endeavored to amplify children's voices as legitimate addressees (Henward, 2015) and consider aspects of democratic and emancipatory early childhood education (Skarpenes & Sæverot, 2018). Therefore, the aesthetic dimension has already been inherent to many ethnographic researches in childhood studies yet have not been recognized enough, especially through Rancièrian lens. It is my hope that, therefore, through highlighting the essential aesthetic aspect of ethnography and practicing the presumption of equality in our relationships with children, we *do* something differently in our methodological and relational approaches to the study of children.

An Aesthetico-Ethnographic Case Study

Event #2. Ayla, Leah, and Austin were drawing individually at the art table. I found Leah's drawing of female figures quite interesting and made a note about this in my sketchbook. Ayla jumped to come close to me and recognized Leah's name. "Where's my name?" she asked. "Right here," I responded, pointing to Ayla's name written in my sketchbook. She asked what I had written about Leah. I slowly read the note "Leah asks me to draw an image of a girl she found on my iPhone." After listening carefully, Ayla asked me what the word "image" means. I answered that it is like "a picture." She was also curious about why I was taking notes, to which I responded, "Because I want to keep a record of what happened and remember it." Ayla then demanded, "You should also write about Austin." Without hesitation, I agreed, "Yeah, I should" and wrote Austin's name in my sketchbook page.

Field notes, February 6, 2018

Attending to the potential aesthetic unfoldings in the process and product of ethnography, I consider the research methodology for this research to be an aesthetico-ethnographic case study, primarily for two reasons: the length of the fieldwork and the underlying objective of the research. Because my ethnographic fieldwork was conducted for eight months, visiting 3 hours per week, I am hesitant to describe my work as a traditional ethnography, as ethnographers typically immerse in the field for at least one year[2] engaging in everyday activities with the participants. In my case, I visited the site twice a week, which allowed only a partial observation of children's everyday events in the classroom. However, despite my relatively short engagement in the research site, I was able to build rapport with child participants and attain a sense of understanding about the explicit and subtle dynamics present in the kindergarten classroom community. It was through this ethnographic approach that allowed me to capture the voices of children and thereby contextualize their lived experience that "goes beyond mere fact and surface appearances," which "presents details, context, emotion, and the webs of social relationships that join persons to one another" (Denzin, 1989, p. 83).

Inasmuch as my study is primarily a theoretical work that examines Rancière and other thinkers' ideas in the context of early childhood art education, my focus is in doing the theoretical exploration *through* the specific events I encounter at the kindergarten classroom. In other words, the documentations described in this book contribute as examples to actively think *with* and *through* the politics and aesthetics of children's art, pedagogy, and ethics, rather than to serve as mere "data." Another aim in the study of children's work and lives is not to make definitive generalizations *about* them but to present particularities of children's experience *with* and *alongside* them. As such, along with the observational and participatory methods of ethnography, my research also espouses that of a case study, an exploration of a bounded system (i.e., kindergarten classroom) or a case (or multiple cases) over time through in-depth study within the specific context that might be highly pertinent to the knowledge of individual, group, organizational, social, political, and related phenomena of study (see Creswell & Poth, 2018; Stake, 2005; Yin, 2014). Describing what it means to be "on the case," Dyson and Genishi (2005) write:

> It is the messy complexity of human experience that leads researchers to case studies … They identify a social unit, for example, a person, a group, a place or activity, or some combination of those units—a child's city block perhaps: that unit becomes a case of *something*, of some phenomenon.
>
> (p. 3)

It is precisely the appeal of "messy complexity" that my research yearns to attend to—the complex entanglement of materials, relationships, politics, and culture that surround the case of children's art in the kindergarten classroom.

Particularly, I see "case(s)" happening in two ways in my research: first, from a holistic sense of qualitative methodologies studying a singular phenomenon it is an ethnographic *case* study of children's art in a preschool classroom. Second, what constitutes the case study are multiple *cases* of children's artistic events, where each event is considered as a distinct case. Although this might be similar to the characteristics of "embedded cases" (Yin, 2014), where the researcher can choose to make a single case study with embedded subunits that are located within a larger case, I refrain from such labeling in order to sustain my intention to highlight each artistic event as a cultural manifestation, one that exceeds the idea that children's art is a "thing" subject to be arranged under a larger study. In other words, each art event attains children's visual cultural knowledge beyond the confinements of the classroom setting—it is a performative practice where lived experiences emerge and converge. For example, the event above of drawing Moana characters function as *a case*. Sophie's personal history of watching the animated film and her appreciation of the characters, to the degree of wishing to represent the figures in drawing, implies that her lived experiences outside of the kindergarten classroom extend and conjoin at the site of an art table. Yet it was not only Sophie's observation and understanding of the characters but also Katie and Zoey's, and even my lived experiences and cultural knowledges, that converged in visual and narrative forms upon the provocation of a particular media content.

As such, I view each artistic event *more than* a submissive unit that serve for a broader inquiry. In the following chapters, I bring up two distinct cases that invoke different aspects of children's art. I trouble each case through multiple contexts, from the topic of children's resistance to adult assumptions to the ethics that concerns the relationship between the researcher and children. Thus, this aesthetico-ethnographic case study aims to investigate how the theories associated with childhood and children's art enlivens in reality and how children make sense of it through the observation and participation in the socio-cultural-political site.

In order to make a point on aesthetic ethnography that is on the basis of equality, it is essential to consider how ethical and representational ethnography might look like and whether these events would be considered as data. As Rancière (2004b) describes the representational regime of art identified within the *mimesis/poiesis*, that of "forms of know-how" and "imitations or arrangements of represented actions" (p. 65), I argue that ethnographic studies in the representational regime would be the ones concerned about the principles of distinction and comparisons, relying on specific criteria of identification and predicated on some notion of inequality. Though anthropologists originally developed ethnography as a research approach that attempts to understand and describe other cultures, it is no secret that the method has been closely associated with the study of the Other and the defining of primitivism (Stocking, 1987). Further, the ethnographic gaze of anthropology has often "collected, classified and represented other cultures" (Smith, 2012, p. 70) to the extent that indigenous people perceive anthropologists as "bad" and exploitative. Research with children, too, have *not* been so aesthetic, but rather predicated on some notion of inequality and hierarchy. Despite the paradigm shift in the social study of childhood from traditional research methods to relational and participatory approaches, the employment of testing, measurement, or two-way mirror observations is still commonly practiced in studies of childhood and children's world. This is because the access itself often constructs children as "others" and extends the unequal relationship between children and adults. In this sense, it is very likely that the events I describe here would not be considered as valid data in the representational regime of art, as it is not overtly classifiable into arrangements of represented actions. For ethnographic research to be aesthetic, therefore, it would be critical to challenge dominant methods that merely perpetuate asymmetrical relationships. Some examples of aesthetic methods could be using audio, photographic, and video recording data as well as descriptive field notes or vignettes, along with the researcher's will to ground equality as premise of the research relationship. I have endeavored to embrace such methods and attitudes in my aesthetic ethnographic study, which will be further described in the following.

Revisiting my exchange with Sophie in Event #1, I view that, even within the short exchange, an aesthetic aspect unfolds as the process of my trying to know children's culture strays away from searching for the one-right-truth. The pre-existing truth I carried in this case was the idea that Maui couldn't possibly be something else than a geographical location—an immediate assumption that fails to escape my own set of knowledge. However, Sophie's simple response "No, Maui" challenged my presumptions, implying that there is something else called Maui, a character that was in fact so obvious and integral to the visual culture of children's everyday lives. My static, definitive idea of Maui foolishly collapsed and searched for means of redemption: the introduction to new knowledge. This process allowed me to disrupt my own conception on children's culture, particularly their production and consumption of media culture, even the ones I thought I was knowledgeable about.

Event #2 invites me to think about "leakages" (Cornwall & Park, 2022) in research, especially in how the binary of "the researcher" and "subjects" gets to be reimagined. Though I initially considered the sketchbook as a container for "data," primarily in texts, it developed into a material of provocations and an open collaborative site for drawing in which methods of ethnography leaked. Though my sketchbook for field notes were initially meant to contain knowledge and experience, one that often holds the authority of confidential information of the research, it began to leak. It opened a site to ponder on how blurring the lines of ownership as children actively contributed to the unfoldings of happenings. As seen in the vignette, there was no neat distinction between my activity of collecting data and engaging with children. Rather, it was an entangled matter where children were active contributors to making the data as they discovered the affordances of the sketchbook. In fact, my few attempts to actually use the notebook for note-taking drew more attention, often resulting in sharing the contents with children. The leakages happened not only in the attempts to collect data, particularly in written field notes, but also in my positionality as a researcher and children's role as participants. The pages were out of order. The data/information in the sketchbook was no longer confidential, and, in fact, directed by the children. The authorship of the contents was no longer solely belonged to the adult researcher but the children as well. Children became researchers, creating field notes and *making* data. This is what I consider as aesthetico-political in this research method—the will of both adult and children to let go the assumed roles and rules to follow in conducting research. We were both participants and researchers.

Moreover, here in the ethnographic writing that describes this specific event, I labor to disrupt the hierarchical role of the researcher and research participants so that an amplification of children's voices could be attained rather than an imposition of my own knowledge in translating the dialogue. Although the one who writes about this event is still the privileged adult, myself, I believe that something different could be produced when the writing actively considers children as legitimate participants who willfully voice themselves, tell interesting stories about their culture, and be skillful writers of their experiences. To continue this thread of thought, in the following chapters where I describe vignettes more extensively, I take the position of the storyteller whereby I interpret the kindergarteners' complex artistic experiences on the basis of aesthetico-ethnographic practices.

Unpacking the Researcher's Membership

In the time span of October 2017 to May 2018, I visited the kindergarten classroom at a childcare center affiliated to and located at the campus of The Pennsylvania State University. This was the only kindergarten class in the Center, while pre-kindergarten and infant/toddler ages consisted of four classrooms each. I visited the classroom twice a week, for up to 1.5 hours each, except for University and National holidays. For the first two months, I visited once in the morning when children participated in activities let by teachers' instructions that relate to a particular topic they discussed as a whole group, and once in the afternoon when children engaged in choice-based activities, dispersed into multiple centers. I observed and participated in naturally occurring activities, from whole-group activities (e.g., book reading, playground time) to small-group centers that usually consisted of Legos, art, reading/writing, math, play areas. Parents of sixteen children consented to my research protocol, where I indicate that I will be taking audio, photographic and video documentation, as well as descriptive field notes. Therefore, in this book I do expose children's facial images; however, I use pseudonyms for all children's names.

As "Integrated Arts Kindergarten," the kindergarten embraced a unique curriculum that juxtaposes the arts to all learning. Accordingly, the classroom environment comprises displayed images of artists' artworks of a wide variety as well as students' works that changed regularly based on the curriculum. Seventeen students of age four to five attended the kindergarten class and there were at least three full-time teachers present everyday: the two classroom teachers, Ms. Joanne and Ms. Carla, and one undergraduate student teacher/ intern per semester from the university. Also, some short-term visitors were occasionally present to observe the classroom: undergraduate students from art education or early childhood education courses, as well as researchers, like myself, who visited more frequently for longer periods. Although the teachers were not participants of my research, I mention their names (also pseudonyms) in this book as their presence played a significant role in children's art making and the verbal exchanges associated with it. Inasmuch as I wished to learn about the classroom culture, rules, power dynamics, activities, relationships, etc. from the perspective of children, I refrained from having too much contact with other adults in the classroom, including other researchers or parents.

As suggested in the opening vignette, children noticed my drawing ability fairly quickly and asked me to draw on the notebook I carried with me for taking field notes. The kindergarteners' desire to draw on my notebook persisted throughout the entire eight months. Upon my arrival, the children were often quick to make this request: "Can I draw on your sketchbook?" or "Could you draw me a princess on your notebook?" Because it was something I had always brought with me, even to the playground, my arrival to the classroom also meant the time to draw on my notebook, particularly with my pen, accompanied with the Google image search tool from my iPhone. Using internet on my phone often worried me in that it would interrupt the teacher's lesson plan or classroom rules. However, the teachers did not seem to mind that the children used my phone and notebook. After completing the drawings, some children wished to tear it off from the notebook and take it home or gift it to friends or teachers. I listened to the stories involved in the drawing, if there were any, and asked permission to take pictures before being taken away. As such, a large portion of my visual documentation portrays children using my notebook drawing a variety of figures, from individual work to collaborative works with peers or with myself.

I realize that how I claimed my role to be in the kindergarten classroom—or how I wanted my role to be understood—and how children perceived my role could be comparatively dissimilar. While the children regarded me as an artist in residence, I entered the kindergarten classroom wishing to embody the role of an interested adult—one who participates in the ongoing everyday lives of children with curiosity, not as one who brings superior (or inferior) knowledge from outside. Thorne (1993) writes about adopting a different role in children's spaces:

> I claimed the free-lancing privilege of an adult visitor. I could, and did, come and go, shift groups … choose and alter my daily routines. Unlike the kids, I was relatively, although not entirely, free from the control of the principals, teachers, and aides … without a fixed school-based routine, I also had more spatial mobility than the teachers or aides.
>
> (p. 14)

As an adult visitor, I wished to become the children's friend who would play, draw, and engage in their everyday activity together. However, being an adult visitor who is neither teacher nor parent was more of a complex matter. In order to stray away from enforcing rules or resolving problems, I had to be aware of such classroom rules so that I can choose *not to* act like a teacher or a parent. I often wondered: how could I negotiate the boundaries of being an adult and that of a friend, since an interested adult, "the least-adult" (Mandell, 1988), or "an unusual adult" (Christensen, 2004), is still an adult?

These boundaries of being the adult in children's spaces demand an understanding of membership roles in the classroom. A researcher's membership role for fieldwork varies on a spectrum, choosing and adapting the types of roles with participants. Sociologists Patricia and Peter Adler (1987) categorize three possible roles a researcher falls into: the peripheral, active, and complete membership role. As an "adult visitor," I partook different memberships in the kindergarten classroom. Casting myself in the *peripheral membership* role, which is to "refrain from participating in activities" (Adler & Adler, 1987, p. 36), during the first several visits I endeavored to familiarize myself with the time structure, space, and materials of the classroom. More importantly, I focused on getting to know with the children by closely observing their peer interactions and class activities without interrupting the nature of events. Then, I gradually allowed myself to immerse into the classroom culture embracing an *active membership* role, that is, to attempt to play and interact with children but not as a member of the group. In building rapport with children, the relationships were much affected by our distinctive cultural contexts, characteristics, and experiences, however, ultimately took the direction of forming friendships.

When a researcher enters the space of children, not only the adult makes sense of children in the culture, but children also make sense of the adult (Knupfer, 1996). The kindergarteners were adept in recognizing my multiple identities, particularly the ostensibly apparent attributes, I carried along with me into the space: being an Asian woman, a graduate student researcher, and a young adult who was not a parent. The first question I was asked on my first day of observation was whether I was somebody's mom, as children recognized the presence of a new adult and her role in the classroom. I was also asked several times why I was coming to the classroom, which I would answer, "Because I want to know about you!" or "I want to play and make art with you." After the fact that I am a student at the university was verified, the next most frequently asked question was in regards to my ethnicity; For example, questions such as "Are you Chinese?" "What are you?" "Can you speak Korean?" were raised. My Asian-ness affected the interactions with children to a certain extent, perhaps more so with students from Asian families. This influenced me to become more cognizant of my positionality as an Asian person researching at a predominantly white classroom for a study that concerns philosophies and methods that Western, white, male scholars developed. Though I remain critical of this reality, I also respect it for allowing me to continuously question my positionality and recognize other minoritized groups of people. As much as the culturally specific identities are highly important, my position as an adult compels me to think about my positionality in the kindergarten classroom more so, as it is subject to produce power dynamics within the relationship with children in virtually any circumstances.

Despite my desire to attain equal status with children through the *complete membership role*, or "the least-adult role" (Mandell, 1988), two main attributes of myself precluded my becoming of the complete member: the skill to draw and the limited knowledge of children's media culture. As my drawing abilities were perceived as "skills that were useful to them" (Corsaro, 2003, p. 31), children perceived my role as that of an artist in residence who is available to draw various figures anytime upon request. In the beginning, I was asked to draw general figures of princesses in which children directed me to include specific features such as hair length, facial expression, or the number of points on the crown. As more children recognized my artistic skills, requests to draw media characters prevailed during every visit. However, when it came to kids' culture, my status as a skillful artist immediately dropped: My drawing abilities couldn't function without external assistance. I was unfamiliar with most of children's contemporary media culture and often was unable to grasp what the children were referring to. Though I was somewhat familiar with their interest in long-standing media (e.g., Barbie, Disney, Star Wars, and Pokémon characters), it was the recent animated children's television series (e.g., PAW Patrol, Super Wings, Vampirina, etc.) that ultimately disclosed my lack of information.

Even when I ventured to proudly present knowledge about certain popular culture contents, it was meager compared to children's proficiency, as the story of drawing Maui portrays. My minimal knowledge in children's popular culture was often revealed during my engagements with children in everyday conversations and activities. Yet, children willingly filled the cultural gap by providing contextual information. In fact, though I might not have attained the complete membership role, I used "emic" interpretations, which is to understand narratives, matters, and cultural events from the participants' point of view, rather than "etic" interpretations, which is to understand the culture from the researcher's perspective (Geertz, 1973).[3] This was possible by making my way through the classroom milieu, mingling in the dynamics of children's everyday lives. Graue and Walsh (1998) observe that the data of studying children not only concerns children in context, but also grasps the researcher in context:

> If research is a process of soaking and poking we emphasize the poking over the soaking ... the researcher is not a fly on the wall or a fog in the pocket. The researcher is there. She cannot be otherwise. She is in the mix.

(p. 91)

There I was, in the mix of children's everyday events, trying to make sense of a snippet of their complex cultural world inextricably entangled with both the adults' and their own values and beliefs.

In retrospect, it is clear that participant observation was far from being solely my own practice. My actions taken as part of the fieldwork were deeply contingent on the children's acceptance of my presence and invitation to be part of their worlds. Moreover, my carrying the notebook and using it for drawing with children allowed the observation be in the *making*, akin to what Springgay and Zaliwska (2015) calls "data-in-the-making" (p. 142). Though sharing a tool for data collection with children was far from my initial plan, it was evident that the notebook became a collaborative site for drawing with children, where cultural knowledges and lived experiences converged. The openness to children's voices allowed the researcher to resist asymmetrical distributions of normalized research methods, which contributed to attaining the aesthetic dimension of this study.

Throughout the aesthetico-ethnographic case study, I aspired to be present and attentive to children's stories, actions, and thoughts in the visual cultural engagement, being simultaneously cognizant of my adult researcher positionality. I focused on the aesthetic aspects of ethnographic practice in children's everyday events, doings, and the relations with their surrounding materials or humans, similar to what Vannini (2015) described as attributes of nonrepresentational research. What I suggest through my aesthetico-ethnographic case study is a kind of relational and ethical approach, among many, to think differently about the researcher-participant dynamics in researching with children. The practice of relational ethics in researching with children will be further discussed in Chapter 5, along with a story about drawing popular culture figures in the kindergarten classroom.

"Out of the Lines": The Politics and Aesthetics of Oliver and Brian's Art Making

If emancipatory politics could emerge anywhere and anytime (Biesta, 2008), how might politics come about in the everyday spaces of early childhood education? And, as politics rests on "dissensus" (Rancière, 2015), what ghostly policing conditions do children disagree with as a community of political subjects? I inquire about these questions by situating my observations at the kindergarten classroom within a theoretical illustration that consists of Rancièrian and other poststructural lines of thought. Whereas the previous chapters *told* of the theories about the distribution of the sensible and the politics in art education, here, I attempt to *show* how such politics might come into being, especially in early childhood spaces where children engage in art making. Continuing the exploration of politics, subjectivization, and aesthetics, below I present a painting event I encountered while at the kindergarten classroom in order to discuss how young children engage in politics as political subjects, who participate in, disagree with, and negotiate the assumptions that haunt their artistic practice. In what follows, I interrogate this event by focusing on two conceptual elements: the aesthetics of *politics* and the politics of *aesthetics*. In doing so, it is my attempt to further complicate and recontextualize the often simplified and decontextualized understandings that exist about children's art, and thus produce new and different perspectives toward the politico-aesthetic performances of young people.

Event: Brian, Oliver, and the Big Black Dots

On a Friday afternoon of January, center time opens up. Inspired by George Seurat's pointillism technique, Ms. Carla prompts a painting activity at the art table. She takes out a canvas pre-painted in diagonal lines, in which children were expected to fill the divided sections with small dots. Brian and Oliver join the art table and choose six different colors of acrylic paint: red, yellow, pink, blue, green, and black. Having the boys and myself gathered around the table, Ms. Carla carefully paints a few dots at the corner of the canvas using a thin paintbrush. The dots are small and in different colors, too. Attentive to Seurat's method, she demonstrates how the dots should be painted close to each other without being mixed, and that the size and the colors of the circles could vary.

After Ms. Carla leaves the art table, Oliver and Brian, sitting across from each other, begin to paint dots on the canvas, rendering different sizes of circles. With his paintbrush carefully touching the surface of the canvas, Brian says, "Look how tiny my dot is, you can't even see it." Oliver draws a circle close to 1-inch in diameter—bigger than the circles Ms. Carla had drawn. Then, he asks me, "Can you see that?" I reply, "That's a huge one!" Oliver's tone rises with excitement, "Oh no, that's a huge, huge, huge, huge, HUGE one!" Utterances emerge and crisscross between Oliver and Brian as they experiment with painting different sized dots.

The boys are laughing, singing, and making unidentifiable noises together while delineating bigger shapes of black dots, *over* the diagonal lines. As they proceed, different colors of paint begin to touch the boys' hands and smocks. Brian recognizes the paint marks covered on his hands. He shows his hands to Oliver, which Oliver responds to, "Hands, hands!" Then Brian adamantly yelled, "Bad hands!" Oliver looks down at his smock that is also covered with paint, while Brian continues to examine his hands, still crying "My hands!" Shortly after, Ms. Carla redirects them to be in control with the paint, and the boys resume painting big black dots.

Oliver discontinues the whirling of the paintbrush saying, "I don't think Ms. Carla's going to be happy about this." Oliver verbally agreed, "Yeah, I don't she's going to be happy." But as he enthusiastically whirled the paintbrush to form a bigger dot, his action seemed to be in conflict with their concern. Brian repeated his previous statement again, "Ms. Carla's not going to be happy. Oh no, oh no." Oliver responds, "And this," followed by laughter.

Brian then eyed Ms. Carla, tracking her movement in the classroom. He then whispered, "Oh, she's coming," and then again, with relief, "Oh, she isn't." In contrast with this concern, and continuing to make bigger dots, Oliver's tone heightened, "Oh no, this is going to be way big, big, big, BIG!" Then, Brian confirms, "Oh no, Ms. Carla's close to us." Now Ms. Carla is actually walking toward the art table. When Ms. Carla approaches the table, Greg, who later joined the activity, carefully asks her, "Do you like the big dots of black?" She replied, "I do." Abruptly turning back and looking at the other boys, Greg exclaimed, "She likes the big dots of black!" In response, Brian says, "I did the bigger one!" And Oliver says, "No, I did. I did the bigger one." Recognizing the tension, Ms. Carla intervened, saying, "Let's not get carried away—an artist has an idea, right?" Despite her comment, Oliver shouts, "I did the big, big, one!"

As Ms. Carla walks away, in a lower voice, Oliver notes, "I messed up the pattern like that," which to me, seemed like a confident claim to make, especially among his peers. At this moment, I quietly ask the boys, "So why did you guys think Ms. Carla wouldn't like the big dots?" Brian responds, "She actually said she did." I asked why he thought she wouldn't like it *before* that, which Oliver answers, "Because they are so big and the other ones are not—because it's *out of the lines*." As the boys' energy for the painting escalated, the pressure given to the paintbrushes forced the end to split in a rake-like shape, which makes louder giggles and exclamations. Shortly after, Ms. Carla returns to the table and comments, "Oh, that is awesome! I like it." The children continue with their previous endeavor of painting bigger dots with loud laughter.

"I think Ms. Carla's going to like it" Brian says. I say, "Maybe … why is that?" Brian responds, "Because black is the blue and the yellow is in the yellow." Meanwhile, Oliver continues to entertain himself by mixing paint "Ahhh! Ha-ha-ha!" The boys also begin to sing. "I think Ms. Carla's going to like it" Brian repeats, and at the same moment, Ms. Carla comes and says, "That is awesome!" Because Oliver continued to paint without following the directions, Ms. Carla says: "Oliver, listen, if you're going to be silly, you need to be done with this job. I want you to do a nice job." Still, Oliver doesn't seem to change the way he paints. Ms. Carla calls him to attention again: "Are you in control of your art? There's a difference between putting some energy in art versus not in control. There's a famous Japanese artist who throws pockets of paint and throws it to the wall. It's pretty cool—it punches walls." Brian jumps in, asking, "Is Oliver trying to do that?" and she responds, "Well, we can study that artist. I think you guys, especially, would enjoy it. Just be careful, okay?" Though Oliver remained quiet during Ms. Carla's comment, after she left, he continued to mix paint intentionally, but in a gentler manner. Shortly after, I was pulled away to the other side of the classroom to draw bunnies and princesses for Lena and Iris. In the meantime, the painting event had come to a closure.

Admittedly, this is an event that could occur in any early childhood setting. The teacher used a conventional representational approach of referencing a historically renowned artist to introduce an art technique, using the everyday classroom art materials, and even children's rebellious or playful acts could commonly emerge in teacher-led activities (Barblett et al., 2016; Shayan, 2022). Nonetheless, I bring my attention to this event *because of* this ordinariness—to see how the very common and subtle moments provoke avenues of inquiry for a broader range of perspectives, bringing into view what elusive forces affect children in their art practices. Importantly, it is not my intention to demonize art educators who subscribe to a particular set of aesthetic standards and instructional methods nor to criticize Ms. Carla's response to the boys' approach on the activity that she set for them to complete. In fact, in this event, Ms. Carla did not disapprove the boys' out-of-the-line painting. Although she did assign a project that aligned with prescribed styles and representational approaches

Figure 1 Brian (right) shows his hands covered with paint to Oliver (left), which Oliver responds to, "Hands, hands!". Then Brian says, "Bad hands!".

Figure 2 Oliver looks down at his smock that is also covered with paint, and Brian looks at his hands.

Figure 3 While Oliver exclaims "Ahh!" Brian cries "My hands!" and Oliver laughs.

to art making, she did not enforce it at all. The point is that Oliver and Brian certainly expected her to do so, *assuming* that the disobedience to the distributed rules and roles would result in unpleasant consequences, as seen in calling their painted hands "bad hands" and the worrisome statements. This assumption is what I focus on complicating in my research and consider as policing—namely, that the boys' assumption that it *would be* enforced and any resistance to the assumption, the big black dots painted out of the lines, would not be tolerated.

Figure 4 The completed work seen in the classroom weeks later (I speculate that other kindergarten students have also contributed to the painting, given that Ms. Carla had introduced the activity as a collaborative painting for the end of the year exhibition).

I take the journey to examine this politico-aesthetic event inviting Rancière as a thinking companion. For Rancière, art and politics do not reside in two distinct realities but in two forms of distribution of the sensible, where both are contingent on a particular regime of identification, as he states, "There are not always occurrences of politics, although there always exist forms of power. Similarly, there are not always occurrences of art, although there are always forms of poetry, painting, sculpture, music, theatre, and dance" (Rancière, 2004b, p. 26). Given Rancière's definitions of politics and art as a persuasion of equality, this quote suggests that genuine politics and art only exists when there is a "rupture in the order of things" (Rancière, 2003, p. 219)—a dissensual act that destabilizes the distribution of the sensible. Both art and politics, in this sense, is neither equitable with the representational forms nor occur on a daily basis. In other words, arts and politics are seldom seen in everyday lives inasmuch as it requires to be *more-than,* or emancipate from, the usual representational forms and partitions bodies are assigned to. As such, I view the painting event more than a form of mundane activities in children's art thus take the responsibility to contribute to amplifying the politico-aesthetic story to be seen and told.

With this ethical obligation, I explore the painting event by bringing my attention to two aspects: One is the *politics* Oliver and Brian attended to, whereby a sense of tension and thrill was demonstrated as a community, and the other is the *aesthetic* experience that was being produced in conjunction with the political enactments. Here, though politics and aesthetics are ultimately homologous to each other for interrupting the distribution of the sensible, I attend to Rancière's differentiation of politics and aesthetics: He describes the paradox of art and politics, with each defining a different form of dissensus, as the aesthetics of *politics* attends to the distribution of the sensible through the "political processes of subjectivation," while the politics of *aesthetics* "lies in the practices and modes of visibility of art that re-configure the fabric of sensory experience" (Rancière, 2015, p. 148). In other words, the former attends to the act or performance of becoming subjects, whereas the latter resides in the *re*-distribution of the sensible of art experiences. As such, in inquiring into the painting event, I explore how Oliver and Brian engaged in political subjectivization and generated affects of reconfiguring sensory experience in what has traditionally been considered as children's art.

The Aesthetics of *Politics*

A Political Subjectivization

As described in Chapter 1, "subjectivization" (Rancière, 1992, 2013a) exists upon the gap between the identity assigned by the police that generates a division of activities in a society and the subject identity the bodies wish to become. In other words, the political subjectivization of those with "no parts" (Rancière, 1999) entails a deliberate disagreement to the given identity that moves toward the constitution of equality between the disparate identities. In this sense, Oliver and Brian painting out of the lines resonates with the process of subjectivization as it reveals three main characteristics of subjectivization—argumentative demonstration, theatrical dramatization, and heterologic disidentification (Davis, 2010, p. 84).

To begin with, the painting event presented an "argumentative demonstration" (Davis, 2010) of political subjectivization, insofar as Oliver and Brian's verbalization and actions strove to attain a sense of equality. I see this as a practical and artistic argument of intellectual equality toward the system of hierarchy that involves a power figure (i.e., adult) and the myth of explication (i.e., instructions to render representational art). It is practical for its alternative form to a formal declaration of equality (e.g., legal documents) that produced an event that brought their presence into visibility by utilizing their given materials and space. Also, in creating a scene of dissensus that affected other agents to pay attention to the occurrence (e.g., Greg, myself, and Ms. Carla) the painting event certainly constituted a "theatrical dramatization" (Davis, 2010). Within the normalized space of the kindergarten classroom art table, the acts of Oliver and Brian going out of the given rules and roles produced a manifestation of a new "subject" that was not expected to exist. It was a pretense of the other—pretending to be *more* than the assigned less-than identity they are often made to uphold as children. The third characteristic of political subjectivization, a "heterologic disidentification" (Davis, 2010), is at the core of this painting event: Oliver and Brian dislocated their given identity that is expected to follow the demonstration and asserted the other identity of being the other, to have equal visibility and audibility as those who impose rules and roles onto them (i.e., adults). It was an "impossible identification" (Davis, 2010, p. 87) yet productive political enactment for its attempt to reveal their "hybridity" (Haraway, 1991) despite the unsettlement and struggle constituted by the process of political subjectivization.

Children live in the reality that their engagement with anything, even with activities designed to for purposes that are creative and playful, requires them to produce an end result that shows their progress and obedience to adults, which accompanies a recurring fear of disapproval and disappointment. What Oliver and Brian feared is the method of explication, which Jacotot refused to comply with when teaching his students *Télémaque*. It is the "myth of pedagogy" (Rancière, 1991) that merely stultifies students through its separation between intelligences— to have one intelligence subordinated to the other. Because this myth of teaching is such a commonly practiced method in education, it is also deeply ingrained as the "usual" way of learning, which children internalize from a very young age. Though my argument may derive from personal observation of the kindergarten children, it is, in fact, consistent with the hauntology of art education that has influenced children's drawing throughout history. As such, in exploring the politics and aesthetics in the following sections, it is this assumption or elusive presence of police in children's art that I bring my attention to, rather than Ms. Carla's instructions or the kindergarten class's curriculum.

Tensions and Thrills in the Process of Subjectivization

I find that there are multiple layers of tensions in the painting event: tensions between adult's instruction and children's own pleasure, between children's assigned identity and desired identity, and between the "proper" use of given materials and experimented methods of engaging with human to nonhuman materials. These tensions materialized into bodily movements and verbalizations, which is precisely what Rancière (1999) defines as subjectivation, "the production through a series of actions of a body and a capacity for enunciation not previously identifiable within a given field of experience, whose identification is thus part of the reconfiguration of the field of experience" (p. 35). Similar to emancipation, the logic of subjectivation is, therefore, a process by which political subjects extract themselves from the dominant partitions of identification and classification.

Oliver's exhilarated utterances of "I messed up the pattern like that," "Because they are so big and the other ones are not," and "Because it's out of the lines," as well as Brian calling his painted hands "Bad hands" suggest their reconfiguration of the dominant order as political subjects—their renditions show an *accidentally deliberate* deviation from the assigned rules and boundaries. I use the paradoxical term "accidentally deliberate" to emphasize that children's dissensual acts are not entirely involuntary nor planned ahead of time, but something that emerges in response to the police's force that affects the production of dissensual acts. The assumed identity as empty operators having no title in the distribution of the sensible was subverted upon Oliver and Brian's intentional dissensus, as they voiced themselves to challenge the given rules of doing and being. It was a search for emancipation that is attainable through the minorities' own effort to divert from their given status and prove that "they are capable of opposing reason with reason and giving their action a demonstrative form" (Rancière, 1995, p. 48). As such, as the kindergarteners lingered with the tensions that arose as they removed themselves from the naturalness of a place and the identity expected to follow instructions ordered by the adult(s).[1]

Oliver and Brian not only struggled together in disrupting the assigned conditions that confine their sensible experience, but also shared the *thrill* of transgressing the borders drawn by adults. The utterances of joy, such as "This is going to be bea-u-tiful!" and "Yeah, and this one's going to get really big— wah, wah, wah!" as well as the facial expressions of grins and eye contacts. The vocalized expressions of giggling, singing, and exclaiming that emerged in-between verbalized anxiety also insinuated effects of pleasure, though such moments failed to last long. Their deviance of creating marks that literally and figuratively *crossed* the pre-established boundaries generated simultaneous tension and pleasure—a tension of negotiating between the police order and the pleasure that emerged as they refused the identity imposed by others in the process of subjectivation. Yet they still remain in the liminal space between the assigned identity and the achieved one in their journey of searching for equality.

Acts

Acts are an essential quality of politics for Rancière. In an interview with Mark Foster Gage (2019), he gave the example of Rosa Parks' enactment of subjectivity in Montgomery, Alabama, in which she sat on a seat reserved for whites on a segregated bus and refused to give it up. Rancière referred to her act as a practice of "affirming equality" (p. 22). Rather than simply revealing inequality, the political subject attained her subjectivity through the act of staging the contradiction between opposite identities and creating something new out of the tensions between such parts.

I view Oliver and Brian's expression of pleasure as an *act* of affirming equality as well, of which children encountered as they break with the partitions that function to limit the range and mobility of their immanent performances. In *Acts of Citizenship*, Isin (2008) defines the word "acts" by drawing on contemporary political thought theorist Robert Ware (1973), who distinguishes "act" and "action"[2] and thereby list six necessary conditions for something to be called an act, which I summarize as:

1. To specify an act is to indicate a *doing*: while actions also involve a doing, it necessitates movement, change, and motion of objects and bodies, but the kind of doing that acts indicate is not dependent on objects and bodies;
2. Acts are doings of either human or humanized actors (e.g., acts of nature), while actions can occur without actors;
3. Acts happen because of a decision to perform the act. The decision can be intentional or non-intentional but an act will always involve a decision;
4. Acts take time and space for doing, but do not have spatio-temporal coordinates;
5. Acts involve accomplishments: "Doings that go on for a period of time and that can be continued or broken off might be action or activities [routines or practices], but they are not acts" (Ware, p. 413, as cited in Isin);
6. Acts have continuity within themselves—they accrete over time. (p. 23)

The three entities involved in the definition of acts—acts, actions, and actors—distinguish and emphasize that acts cannot be actualized without actions, the intentional and communal performances of bodies upon the purpose to accomplish something as a result. In focusing on the ontological difference between acts and actions, Isin further attends to philosopher Adolf Reinach (1983), who interpreted the fundamental quality of an act as an expression of the need to be heard (and seen). Investigating various types of acts (e.g., willing, commanding, requesting, and contemplating), Reinach argued that a social act must enact a *need* felt by one party to be heard by another via linguistic or nonlinguistic means, and therefore making acts inescapably dialogical (Reinach, as cited in Isin, 2008).

In this particular event, the act of citizenship was not so much about attaining a status the children didn't have—as they *are* already citizens of the classroom—but rather an act of recognizing and practicing their already-present agency as autonomous artists capable of dismantling the representational order. It is the linguistic or nonlinguistic dialogical methods children utilize as a means to be recognized or heard by adults, a desire that constitutes their social acts. For example, Oliver and Brian's dissensual act reminds us the conditions that acts involve "movement, change, and motion of objects and bodies," and occur because of a "decision to perform the act" (Ware, 1973, as cited in Isin, 2008, p. 23). The performance of painting big dots was entangled with bodily movements (e.g., hand motions and vocalizations) as well as materials affected and altered by the bodies (e.g., paint brushes changing shapes and paints being mixed). This goaded the materials to go out of the lines, to interact with human bodies out of the instructed methods. Because these acts were accidentally deliberate, continuous decision making was involved, to make each move visible and audible. In doing so, their decision to produce movements of changing the order of the distributed sensible created an unusual scene—a "theatrical dramatization" (Davis, 2010). It was a profound performance of political acts.

Further, acts involve "accomplishments" (Ware, 1973). In Oliver and Brian's painting event, I speculate that the accomplishments exist within the performance of going out-of-the-lines, as effects of emancipation. Here, the effects of emancipation entail the experience of the *other* identity: to escape from the lines that were drawn to limit movements; to engage in the hybridity of materials by mixing the paints, rendering paint marks on their bodies, and playing with force given to the paint brushes; and exploring the emotions of exhilaration and simultaneous fear that was produced when fully engaging in these human-material encounters. Perhaps, Ms. Carla's assertion "I like it!" contributed to the momentary release of the haunting assumption that she would disapprove their work. This is only to mention the accomplishments that were visible to me, that were outwardly performed and recognizable. However, since children's art practices contain entangled threads of thoughts, experiences, and relationships, achievements that are invisible to me might have occurred, too.

Acts also have "continuity within themselves" that accrete over time (Ware, 1973, as cited in Isin, 2008, p. 23). In other words, acts reside in the intensity that is produced among the continuous performances. The most apparent act that persisted in the painting event is the sustained performance of rendering bigger dots even after a concern of disapproval was expressed. Canadian philosopher Brian Massumi (2002) describes intensity being "associated with nonlinear processes: resonation and feedback that momentarily suspend the linear progress of the narrative present from past to future" (p. 26). The intensity of creating bigger dots disrupted the anticipated linear progress of painting dots for representing pointillism. It was something other-than painting, or not-painting, that emerged within the process of engaging with given materials and time. Consider how Oliver's act of painting and laughter contrasted to the expression of agreement to Brian's words, as he accelerated the rhythm of the brushstrokes while saying, "Yeah I don't think she's going to like it." It was a deliberate performance and emancipatory enactment manifested as a pleasure in the midst of communicated tensions, which gained intensity as it proceeded.

Here, laughter is another important political operator. Oliver and Brian's laughter emerged as a spontaneous yet transgressive act against the lines and expected ways of painting, as is a type of joy that is produced upon an embodied deconstruction and imagined democratic reality. In fact, according to Lewis (2012), laughter can be seen as "a particular redistribution of pleasure and pain that breaks with the affective void in contemporary schooling practices" (p. 17). Lewis's argument comes from an inversion of Rancière's (2004a) thesis on the politics of writing, where laughter becomes a verification of joy of democracy and further allows a space for dissensus. This is why I consider children's public joy of laughter and the simultaneous expression of anxiety produced a collective enunciation of artistic experience through the *acts* of dissensus.

Community

In thinking about the shared tensions and thrills in painting big dots, the act of going out of the lines did not occur on an individual level but rather within a group of children. That is, the tension involved in Oliver and Brian's process of subjectivization transmitted to Greg, who asked Ms. Carla how she thinks about the painting even though he had joined the art table quite later after the painting had proceeded for a while. Greg was able to immediately recognize what was being *out* of the expected practice and what Oliver and Brian feared about. Together, they measured the gap between their designated identity presumed to abide by adult control, and the new identity capable of painting outside of the given instructions. Being with each other, they verbally communicated the recurring fear of adults' potential control over their work as well as the entertainment of painting bigger dots. Subjectivation, therefore, formulates a sense of community, as Rancière (2015) writes that the aesthetic movement of politics "consists above all in the framing of a *we*, a subject of collective demonstration whose emergence is the element that disrupts the distribution of social parts" (pp. 149–150, original italics). This notion of a "we" contributes to constructing a community of political subjects who challenge their designated social position to demonstrate their equality to those in power—it is a community of no-part. Insofar as "Political being-together is a being-between: between identities, between worlds" (Rancière, 2004b, p. 137), children sharing the in-between identity together constitute a political community of heterogeneity. And, in this community, it involves going *out of* identities that the distribution of the sensible assigned to bodies.

The political tension, in fact, materialized because children are adept in understanding both adults' and children's desires, coping with their in-between status of the two worlds—the children's and the adults'. That is, as social beings living in social environments, children constantly negotiate between the adults' world and their own world (Corsaro, 2015) without dismissing either one. For children, it is impossible to reside in one territory, as just being child or just adult, but are always in the mix of the two identities. In fact, they share the in-between status together, by being between identities and worlds (Rancière, 2004b). Although modern educational approaches encourage children's autonomy to speak, make themselves visible, and to be in control of their own behavior, children are also proficient in noticing how they could be controlled by the subtleties of power and knowledge (Foucault, 1980). The kindergarteners were very much aware of the power and their assigned partition, as the tension between pleasing the adult and their own desire prevailed. Consider Brian's continuous tracking of the teacher's movement as his peers' excitement intensified. Also, his interpretation of painting big black dots depended on the adult's reaction: Ms. Carla's simple response, "I do [like that big dot]," released his concern about disappointing the adult, as his expression changes from "Ms. Carla's not going to be happy about it," to "I think Ms. Carla's going to like it." By cause of the adult's simple affirmation of acceptance, the practice of painting big dots over the lines was not the same as before but rather transferred into an emancipatory artistic performance. Even Oliver, who seemed to be drawn more to his own excitement of painting bigger dots when Brian expressed his concern, was also aware of his expected identity and behavior, given his confident announcement that he had created a bigger one shortly after Ms. Carla's approval. As political subjects, therefore, children measured the gap between the two worlds (the adults' and the child's), negotiated with the desire of each world, and attained a sense of emancipation by traversing the familiar logic.

Children mobilized a community of political subjects that shares their in-between status as a common identity. Rancière (1992) writes that "a [political] subject is an outsider or, more, an *in-between*" (p. 61, original italics) as they are situated in between more than one identity, status, and name:

> Political subjectivization is the enactment of equality—or the handling of a wrong—by people who are together to the extent that they are between. It is a crossing of identities, relying on a crossing of names: names that link the name of a group or class to the name of no group or no class, a being to a nonbeing or a not-yet-being.
>
> (Rancière, 1992, p. 61)

Reiterating Corsaro's (2015) view on children living in two worlds, as in-between beings continuously negotiating the two social realms, political subjectivization of children is the rejection of both a socially determined role and the adoption of an "impossible identification" (Rancière, 1992). Children formulated a community within the process of democratic politics in which those who have no part make the impossible declaration that they are legitimate beings within the whole of the community.

In fact, Rancière (1995) regards democracy as the "community of sharing" in which "a membership in a single world which can only be expressed in adversarial terms, and a coming together which can only occur conflict. To postulate a world of shared meaning is always transgressive" (p. 49). It entails a process of subjectivization in which the presupposition of equality and the transgression of the distribution of the sensible emerge as a contrast to a given police order. Rancière calls this community a "community of equals," which is an "insubstantial community of individuals engaged in the common creation of equality" (Rancière, 1995, p. 84). Insofar as equality is not an endpoint to be reached but a "presupposition" and "practice" (Rancière, 1991), the community of equals does not resemble a form of social institution but is linked to "the act of its own verification" (Rancière, 1995, p. 84). Interpreting Rancière's (1995) statement that community of equals cannot be institutionalized but exist within its *acts*, May (2008) writes:

> Equality exists only in a collective movement, not in anything institutional that frames that movement of arises from it. For a community to be tied to its own act of verification, which is always in need of reiteration, seems to imply that a community of equals exists only in act, never in a static form. We might say here that a community of equals can only be a verb, never a noun. It is a happening rather than a site.
>
> (p. 103)

This resonates with the conditions and characteristics of acts that were discussed in the previous section: acts distinctive from actions for its involvement of movements, change, and continuity, to name a few. It is a community of equals that actively voice themselves against the police order rather than a static group. In this community, bodies of *sans-part* converge and continuously engage in the practice of equality in order to have their presence be recognized and legitimized. In other words, the process of political subjectivization Oliver and Brian collectively engaged in is a process about appearance—"the coming into presence" (Bingham & Biesta, 2010, p. 33)—and its simultaneous disruption to the existing hierarchical order that produces something different, something new, to this naturalized order. In other words, politics only properly emerges through the antagonism of a common sense or a given order, it contains aesthetics at its core to the extent that a redistribution of the sensible is contingent, a shift in public consciousness concerning what is seen and who can legitimately speak.

The Politics of *Aesthetics*

The second aspect I focus on is the *aesthetics* that materialized in the painting event. The "politics of aesthetics" does not indicate political art containing the artist's ideological implications, as Rancière is quite skeptical of such type of political art. Instead, the politics and aesthetics means two compelling possibilities that is recognized as oppositional yet always exist simultaneously within the "aesthetic regime of art" (Rancière, 2004b, 2011, 2013a, 2015)—the collapse of the hierarchical system that controlled the ethical and representational regimes of art. As Rancière argues in *Aesthetics and Its Discontents*, there is "an originary and persistent tension between the two great politics of aesthetics: the politics of becoming-life of art and the politics of resistant form" (2004b, pp. 43–44). In the former, the "becoming-life" of art, art constitutes "new forms of life in common and hence eliminates itself as a separate reality" (Rancière, 2004b, p. 44). Here, aesthetics ultimately denotes equality of the indiscernibility between art and life where the aesthetic experience dissolves into other forms of experiences, into forms of life. It is a re-distribution of the sensible that constitutes the equality of being-in-common, forming a sense of community and collectivity disruptive of the established police order—it generates new forms of thinking, doing, and living. In the latter politics of aesthetics of being in a "resistant form," on the other hand, denotes a sense of retention of such new possibilities, to "[enclose] the political promise of aesthetic experience in art's very separation, in the resistance of its form to every transformation into a form of life" (Rancière, 2004b, p. 44). Works of art that are emancipated from the "proper" forms of sensory connection resist to be dissolved into life or community.

This opposition between art as art and art as life generates a tension that "respond[s] to a *free play*, meaning a nonhierarchical relation between the intellectual and the sensory faculties" (Rancière, 2009c, p. 37, my emphasis). The political contingency of the aesthetic experience, therefore, emerges from the divorce of art from other forms of activity, its resistance to any transformation into a form of life, yet the inclination to associate with such forms of life. The aesthetics thus rests on a paradoxical idea of which art assembles the possibilities to reshape life on the condition that it simultaneously maintains its difference as art. This is what politics on aesthetics means: art and life containing potentials to retain their essential differences yet exchange properties. In this next section, I explore the politics of aesthetics in Oliver and Brian's event by pointing out how the art attended to the free play between art and life, within its politics of going out of the lines.

Dissensus as Free Play

The event of Oliver and Brian constituted a sense of aesthetics that is part of the aesthetic regime of art. Refusing to resemble representational art, they generated a new mode of art and a new form of community, a complicated "system of heterologies" (Rancière, 2013a, p. 60). The distribution of the sensible that formulates ordinary connection between form and matter, appearance and reality, activity and passivity, as well as comprehension and sensibility was disrupted. It was rather a "free play" of the faculties—intellectual and sensible—that established a new community of "out of the lines" by choosing the sensible side of divergent desire thus refuting what the "proper" form of intelligence, to understand and produce by the given instructions. And, the destabilized naturalness of senses constituted an assemblage of tensions and thrills, to the extent that the boys themselves recognized the intensity of doing so. My earlier descriptions of Oliver and Brian's aesthetic engagement as a "painting" event may seem ironic, as I have advocated a disagreement to such labels, as something that does not resemble ordinary modes of painting. However, it is also my intention to explore the meaning and modes of painting without creating a distinction between what is painting and what is not. In other words, I aspire to explore the diversity of definitions that could be generated in thinking about painting as aesthetic experience, especially the aesthetics young people engage in. This unsettling aspect of aesthetics is constitutive of the heterogeneity that disrupts ordinary and expected senses. As such, I continue to use the term painting for describing the vignette above, yet with the aesthetic connotations in mind.

This de-hierarchization between art and life is, in fact, depicted in Rancière's examination of the nineteenth-century French workers in *The Nights of Labor* (1989). As a mode of emancipation, the workers deviated from the social common sense—or the distribution of the sensible— that precluded them as artists or intellectuals. They instead enacted as proletarian intellectuals, poets, and artists who were capable of articulating their thoughts as they gathered to write poems, journals, music, letters, and to discuss issues at night. The workers were migrants who resided in the in-betweenness of statuses, identities, and classes, yet regarded the practice at night as their real life. Likewise, as children are also living in the in-between space, they produced an aesthetic experience when the order of the police loosened. Rancière (2015) argues that "art *is* politics" (p. 180, original italics) not because of the art's way of rescuing, imitating, or anticipating politics, but because it is properly speaking the identity of people. This implies that young people are capable of attaining a sense of equality opposed to the traditional social identity through engaging in art practices despite or *because of* the essential inequality of their biological, social, conceptual differences from adults.

In this sense, the type of art that Oliver and Brian produced resonates with the paradoxical characteristics of the politics of aesthetics, art becoming life and its resistance to become life (Rancière, 2004b). On the one hand, Oliver and Brian's deliberate suspension of representational painting and the strategic "dissensuality" that was activated instead suggests art practice being dissolved into life. Life, here, could entail the everyday matters that children encounter and experiences that may seem mundane and unnoteworthy. However, by bringing art into life, they persistently manifested a rupture of the rules of art and the laws of sensibility throughout this event when the power (i.e., the presence of the adult) slackened, and the pleasure shared in common was taken as verification of suspending the assigned order. On the other hand, the art activity preserved the material difference of art apart from the usual modes of everyday lives, by using the visual medium to declare dissensus instead of highlighting their in-between identity without utilizing the visibility of material performances. This tension between the two is what makes art aesthetic, as

> there is no art without a specific form of visibility and discursivity which identifies it as such. There is no art without a specific distribution of the sensible tying it to a certain form of politics. Aesthetics is such a distribution. The tension between these two politics threatens the aesthetic regime of art. But it is also what makes it function.
>
> (Rancière, 2004b, p. 44)

Therefore, though tensions could be unsettling, lingering with this paradox opens up new perspectives of looking into the politics of aesthetics.

Rancière's emphasis on the equality between art and life in the politics of aesthetics helps understand how children's aesthetic experience is integral to their everyday activity, as they gravitate toward the autonomy of one's *experience* in relation to art in the process of making, more than the *product* of art. This ignorance of the subject matter and the division between art and nonart constitutes a sense of equality between daily life and artistic practice. Brian Massumi (2013) asserts that an art practice can be political in its own way without having any overtly political content. He elaborates:

> It [art] can push further to the indeterminate but relationally potentialize fringes of existing situations, beyond the limits of current framings or regulatory principles. Aesthetic politics is an exploratory politics of invention, unbound, unsubordinated to external finalities. It is the suspensive aspect of it that gives it this freedom. The suspension of the most available potentials, the potentials already comfortingly embodied, well housed and usefully institutionalized, gives a chance for more far-fetched potentials to ripple up. Aesthetic politics is "autonomous" in the sense that it has its own momentum, it isn't beholden to external finalities.
>
> (pp. 53–54)

In this sense, children's aesthetic engagement itself constitutes political forms of thinking, playing, art making, and other intellectual activities associated with diverse matters in everyday life (e.g., objects, people, places, visual culture, and so forth). Oliver and Brian explored how going out of the lines in already-understood appearances can disrupt the governing aesthetics and therefore affect the ways in which they make sense of the world. To reiterate, it suggests that the art making participated in the aesthetic regime of art by producing rupture and interruption to the general distribution of the ways of doing and being, thus constituting a potentially different distribution of the perceptible emerged within the life of children.

Material Encounters

Continuing my focus on the politics of aesthetics, I inquire how materials might have played the role to goad Oliver and Brian to engage in such dissensual painting event. What are the children's interactions that produce something more than representational art and more than sans-part bodies? In other words, how might materials be affective agents capable of constituting dissensus *with* the children? As I look closer, I find that multiple out-of-the-line manifestations can be observed in this aesthetic event: The paint being mixed in the water cups, paints traveling outside the boarders of the canvas and to the boys' hands, and the divergent affects of laughter and fear that were produced performatively. Here, I look into the bodily actions that emerged through the material encounters that occurred: how the materiality of paint, canvas, water, paint brushes, and other entities of the space produced the act of engaging with other—the emotions of fear and joy, performances of swirling and stopping, and the utterances of "ahs" and "oh-nos."

Drawing from a post-humanist perspective, Pacini-Ketchabaw, Kind, and Kocher (2016) investigate how materials in early childhood spaces "speak back" to children in a way that produces "material—discursive relationship" (p. 3) among humans and the material environment that involves objects and spaces. Describing the materials' ability to communicate with humans recognizes materials' agency as equally capable to produce meanings as human agency. Specifically discussing their experience with paint, they write "paint invited bodies to collaborate, to coorporate. It invited forces to interact and interfere with each other" (Pacini-Ketchabaw et al., 2016, p. 46). The materiality of paint invites human bodies to move, change, and interact with one another producing affective avenues. The big black dots Oliver and Brian collaboratively rendered also left traces visually and politically—the marks couldn't be undone. Political enactment leaves traces, as the subjectivization entails bringing into visibility and audibility that was previously unseen and unheard. Within the process of subjectivization, painting invites bodies to perform as a community, specifically as community of *sans-part*, as alliances of political subjects.

Further, Pacini-Ketchabaw et al. (2016) elaborate on children's process of becoming familiar with the materiality of paint: "becoming competent or familiar with paint involves blurring the gap between the manipulations required to use paint in developmentally focused early childhood classroom and those required in the classroom conditions" (p. 51). This resonates with Oliver's and Brian's use of paint being "out of the lines," in which the paint, paintbrushes, hands, and bodies were not moving as told by the instructions: the painted dots were big while they had to be small, the paints were mixed while they were told to be next to each other without touching, the performance of painting was risk-taking while the instruction was to follow the rules of Pointillism, and so on. The boys were blurring the gap between what is a "proper" use of paint and their own way of creating artistic experiences *with* paint. It was an act of re-distributing the distribution of the sensible in the early childhood art practices— to "recompose the world" (Pacini-Ketchabaw et al., 2016, p. 52).

In this sense, seeing how the materials involved in this event actively affected Oliver and Brian's re-distribution of the sensible, I am reminded of Barad's statement that "Agency is not held, it is not a property of persons or things; rather, agency is an enactment, a matter of possibilities for reconfiguring entanglements" (Barad, 2012, p. 55). Although Rancièrian concepts tend to highlight the human agency capable of producing politics of dissensual enactments, I hereby attempt to reconcile the distinction between the perspectives between human-centered engagement and post-humanistic engagement by inquiring what might happen when human actors and nonhuman actors work together affectively. Like *Télémaque* served as the mediator between Jacotot and his students in *The Ignorant Schoolmaster* (1991), art becomes the medium of political enactments between humans and nonhumans. Nonhuman materials contain possibilities to invite and interact with human bodies that result in producing actions. Rather than focusing on the property of materials—of what it is supposed to do—it is a suggestion to think about the innate performativity of materials, to think of what it can do beyond assigned roles and what it can do with other entities. In other words, how might materials go out of the lines, beyond their given identity as materials? If we begin to think about the possibilities along with the possibilities of human agents producing out-of-the-line politics, the variety of works and performances that could be produced as art becomes unlimited. It is a dissensus of which humans and materials do all kinds of activities in suspending the distribution of the sensible.

Lines of Police, Dots of Dissensus, and Shapes of Aesthetics

Images produced by these materials are also significant actors in this event, most noticeably *lines* and *dots*. There were lines pre-drawn by the adults on the canvas surface, lines of the edges of the rectangular canvas, and the invisible lines that established boundaries on the children's activity. It was not only the physical lines but also the ghostly lines that conjured to limit the bodily performance. Also, these lines divided the identity of who gets to give an assignment and demonstrate the rules of an activity, and who is given that explication thus expected to perform in such ways. Rancière (2009d) observes, "by drawing lines, arranging words or distributing surfaces, one also designs divisions of communal space" (p. 91). He says this in the context of design, but further demonstrates how lines could also yield particular distinctions between the senses:

> by assembling words or forms, people define not merely various forms of art, but certain configurations of what can be seen and what can be thought, certain forms of inhabiting the material world. These configurations, which are at once symbolic and material, cross the boundaries between arts, genres and epochs.
>
> (Rancière, 2009d, p. 91)

Lines, in this regard, symbolically formulates configurations between what can be recognized and not within our material world, which was also the case in Oliver and Brian's painting event.

Lines also carry its undeviating orientation even when it is loose or incomplete. As seen in the dotted-lines reading method Rancière experienced, which I described in Chapter 1, Althusser's students were given incomplete sentences to verify their comprehension of the lesson correctly and knowledge on its application. Waiting for the students to restore what is being omitted, the dotted-lines directed students to perform in predictable ways, to fill in the correct answers—or the answer that pleases the master. Even without the presence of the master, the lines forced the students to achieve its completion by "tracing" (Deleuze & Guattari, 1987)[3] the path that has already been discovered. This was a method of explication that separated bodies (e.g., Althusser and his students) and their according activities, which was only generative of limited thinking and doing. As such, these lines drawn by the police order creates a distribution of the sensible.

However, there were *dots* that contributed to the disruption of these lines, the very visible lines of configurations on the canvas. Dots that initially abided by the boundaries of the pre-drawn lines transformed into having bigger presence in visibility and performativity as they diverted out. Rendering small yellow dots to big black dots, Oliver and Brian explored the potentials of dots that were unlimited in size and color. While lines insinuated linear and static performances, dots contained possibilities to mutate in its own, and invite others to converge and become one another. Dots were mixed by colors and generated different performativities that human bodies are capable of. The diversifying dots not only refused to remain in the boundaries of the canvas edges, but also traveled outside, onto Brian's hands and Oliver's smock, as well as in the water containers. As Peter Hallward (2009) writes, "[e]quality refers not to place but to the placeless or the *out of* place, not to class but to the unclassifiable or the *out of* class" (p. 141, my emphasis), it was a profound manifestation of equality that the unidentifiable people—young children—redefined the distribution of the sensible of the ways of doing, being, saying, and making. This provokes a contemplation on the notion of being "out," a removal from a particular place, class, status, or any normalized context that one might find the urge to escape from, which, in the painting event, was the materials that acted as equally capable agents. Dots constituted the re-distribution of the sensible, to be out of the lines and, moreover, became provocations for children to divert out of their assigned identity. In other words, dots enacted as political agents that affected and interacted *with* other political subjects to attend to dissensus.

The children and materials together *shaped* aesthetics, a plane consisting of political enactments of free-playing between art and life. A force that kept the painting to somewhat remain in the representational modes of art existed as Oliver and Brian began by following the lines and traces drawn by the teacher, yet there was also the desire to traverse out of these boundaries of representation, to constitute a new mode of art. They crossed the assigned identities of a not-yet-artists to achieve a more-than status, which the site of aesthetics offered. As Tanke (2011) interpreted, "dissensus creates a stage of politics" (p. 66), a plane that potentiates unbounded acts of politics of aesthetics to emerge. Therefore, when dots move out of the lines, together they construct a plane, one that consists of infinite directions and movements. Planes contain paths of moving lines, lines with breadth. It invites alterations and provocations the ways in which bodies can explore the performativity of the plane. Because planes are constructed on the basis of dissensus, it is political, potentiating a diversity of shapes to emerge.

Ghostly Matters in the Aesthetic Experience

As mentioned earlier, the ghost that haunted Oliver and Brian is not so much Ms. Carla but the assumption they made even before confirming with Ms. Carla that their dissensus would be tolerated. In fact, Ms. Carla's concern was more about their behavior that seemed to be out of control, not about the work done with paint. What the children assumed was a type of punishment or disappointment on painting bigger dots, having the colors mixed, and allowing paint marks on their hands and smocks. Although, fortunately, Ms. Carla's response was "I like it," accompanied with a sense of permission to continue to create bigger dots, their expectations were the opposite. Given Brian's repeated statement "Ms. Carla's not going to be happy about this," it is apparent that the assumption provoked unsettling fear.

I take a moment here to think with Oliver and Brian, how imagining a rejection from the teacher might have felt like for them. The teacher who left shortly after giving the instructions was nevertheless in their sight—she was present in her absence. The two boys, therefore, were cognizant of her presence/absence that still looked over their painting activity. As they tracked her shadow's movement, a verbal communication about whether or not she is approaching persisted. And, as this anxious tracking continued, they predicted a negative response to be given on their work, just the matter of approaching sooner or later. The assumption of disapproval imagined to come through the body of Ms. Carla was the ghost omnipresent right at the moment.

Thinking with the children conjures up my hauntings at the art hagwon: the fear I underwent for drawing an oval shape smaller than I was supposed to. Whereas the kindergarteners' presumption of punishment was invalidated, my haunting assumption was substantiated by an actual confrontation of punishment. The two events are certainly different from the standpoint of discipline and consequence: whereas my case involved physical punishment that brought sheer shame and enforcement to correct the work, the kindergarteners received a positive response from the teacher who favored their out-of-the-line-ness thus brought ease to their anxiety. Yet both events are similar in a way that the omnipresent idea of students having to please adults, to fulfill given instructions and expectations of adults, affected us. This presumption led all of us—Oliver, Brian, my eleven-year-old self—to project a scene of an unhappy master redirecting us to create a "better" work, that may or may not be accompanied by punishment.

Gordon's (2008) definition of ghosts is helpful to understand the two-headed monster of policing and hauntings that the children and I experienced:

> The ghost is not simply a dead or a missing person, but a social figure, and investigating it can lead to that dense site where history and subjectivity make social life. The ghost or the apparition is one form by which something lost, or barely visible, or seemingly not there to our supposedly well-trained eyes, makes itself known or apparent to us, in its own way, of course. The way of the ghost is haunting, and haunting is a very particular way of *knowing* what has happened or is happening. Being haunted draws us affectively, sometimes against our will and always a bit magically, into the structure of feeling of a reality we come to experience, not as cold knowledge, but as a *transformative recognition*.
>
> (p. 8, emphasis added)

The point being is not the actual presence of the master that is haunting us in person, but rather the social implications that accompany the figure who possesses the power to exercise such discipline on us. It is also the hauntology of art education that comes into play, which children are expected to create works that abide by particular aesthetics and artistic behaviors. Again, this is the myth of pedagogy that Jacotot opposed to (i.e., explication), which only perpetuates the idea that a division of intelligence exists among actors. In other words, explication is haunting. Any pedagogical experience without "ignorance" (Rancière, 1991) is haunting, insofar as explanation only shows a linear path for those of *sans-part* to follow. Within this static and unproductive realm of stultification, there is no other way to create meaning. Therefore, in order to produce experience outside of the linear path, dissensus is necessary, which could only be materialized upon the *knowing* of haunting—as a "transformative recognition" (Gordon, 2008, p. 8).

The dotted-lines reading method of Althusser indicated "the presence of the teacher in his absence" (Rancière, 2004a, p. 134). It demanded the students to respond to the "learning" without asking them any questions nor leaving a room for them to ask questions to the teacher. Just like the pages of dotted-lines children were given before the discovery of child art, the pre-drawn lines and dots Ms. Carla exemplified for Oliver and Brian to imitate, as well as the preconceived standard of how to draw a perfect cabbage—converges here with the common thread as the haunting myth of pedagogy. In this sense, Rancière, children of the pre-child-art era, eleven-year-old myself at the art hagwon, and Oliver and Brian, share some degree of haunting experience from the policing educational disciplines.

However, as Dernikos, Ferguson, and Siegel (2019) suggest, being haunted by ghosts does not automatically mean something bad or traumatic. Rather, being haunted by ghosts produces different ways of seeing and being (Gordon, 1997/2008) that are nonlinear and non-habitual modes of engaging with the world. As ghosts continue to haunt us, "they also watch over us, enabling human beings to 'see' anew … For that reason, ghosts deserve our respect, and even our love" (Dernikos et al., 2019, p. 12). Though loving has not been an easy task, I do endeavor to extend my greatest respect to the ghosts that allow me to think of children's aesthetic experiences differently.

I acknowledge that I was extremely fortunate to observe and be part of Oliver and Brian's dissensual event, inasmuch as "politics doesn't always happen—it actually happens very little or rarely" (Rancière, 1999, p. 17). This is especially true in the context of early childhood education classroom, because going *out* of the lines, to attempt political subjectivization, entails taking the risk of breaking rules, causing disappointment to adults, and, in some cases, being punished as a consequence. Subjectivization entails a laborious process: a recognition of the presumed roles, rules, and expectations imposed—or policed—on those with "no parts"; measuring the gap between such orders and the political subjects' own desire to emancipate from the orders; then executing the desire into action. It is a deliberate enactment of disrupting the preconceived notions to voice themselves as legitimate beings. Also, it is confronting the hauntings yet activating the willingness to overcome the haunted notions that persists to conjure up in everyday lives. This is precisely why I am interested in children's political manifestations as it is rare as well as a difficult decision for them. Police in childhood spaces will always continue to exist in the study of childhood art, in ways that control to children within its absence. But the possibility to alleviate the policing force also exists, by enacting dissensus as political agents and, for adults, through recognizing events of subjectivization and dissensus children engage in.

The Ethics of Ignorance in Drawing Companionships

Rancière's radical break from his mentor Althusser and the kindergarteners' dissensus toward the assumption of the police have particular emancipatory acts in common: the pupils overturn the expected responsiveness, which was to accept the teacher's beliefs and instructions, in order to act as political agents. They took the difficult journey of dissociating with the symbol of power in order to attain a sense of equality that was already present yet pending to be proclaimed. Then, what happens to the sixth-grade girl who could not even dare to think of disagreement—let alone enact dissensus—and submitted to the harsh discipline of teachers at the art hagwon? Instead of situating myself in the endless turmoil of regret ad self-pity, I chose to take the route of contemplating what I can do from now on, which, ironically, I find insight from hauntology.

In *Spectres of Marx*, Derrida (1994) considers the concept of time as nonlinear, as "out of joint."[1] In this dislocated time, the past, present, and future is constitutive of one another, with each containing marks of the others—it is the hauntological imageries folding and unfolding beyond the boundaries of space and time (Maddern & Adey, 2008). In this sense, it compels me to believe that my present experiences contain possibilities to alter and reinterpret the traces from the art hagwon, which, in fact, resides in the broader history of child art being policed by developmental models and Western aesthetics. My hauntings have yet to come to an end thus offers possibilities to repair my compliance. As such, my struggle for emancipation is to refuse reproducing similar disciplinary haunts in the educational settings and in any human interactions I put myself into. I set forth a commitment to actively dissent toward perpetuating hierarchical power relations that my presence might habitually produce, and instead attend to the heterogeneity of logic by actively presupposing and practicing equality (Rancière, 1991). Specific to my aesthetico-ethnographic case study at the kindergarten classroom, I acknowledge that I carried with me multiple privileged statuses: as a researcher, a graduate student, and simply being an adult. The effects of emancipation, therefore, could be achieved by inquiring how I activate the willful practice of equality between the researcher-participant, teacher-student, and adult-child relationships.

Attuned to the commitment of rewriting my memory with present and future emancipatory acts, this chapter considers the dance between police orders and politics in art education research, in order to imagine emancipatory pedagogies. Specific attention will be given to disrupting hierarchies predominant in traditional humanist research (e.g., explanatory researcher and passive subject dynamics). In lieu of these partitions, I argue that we place children at the center of research as a means to highlight *their* voices, *their* personal histories, and *their* culture. In doing so, and as an example of amplifying the worlds of children, I discuss the contentious realm of popular culture, which has long been degraded as lacking nutrition for children's cognitive development and education. Then, I bring up a collaborative drawing event with Alex, a five-year-old boy at the kindergarten classroom, to describe how drawing popular cultural figures guided by his steady instruction activated the will of "ignorance" (Rancière, 1991). Lastly, I unpack this event to explore the relational ethics of researching with children, as informed by thinkers such as Rancière (1991, 2016), Bakhtin (1990), and Haraway (2016). Throughout these unfoldings, I reflect on research in the field of art education and suggest how a relational ethics might help us as art educators to rework the current dynamics that structure and mediate our research with children.

Popular Culture in Early Childhood Spaces

In the kindergarten classroom, children's discussions of media culture frequently played a central role in their everyday social activities and art engagements. Though embraced and encouraged in this particular classroom, popular cultural images, generally, have not always been welcomed by adults, especially in early educational settings. It has been a universal controversy between the perspective that regards it as an unhealthy culture that requires adults' strict monitoring and more tolerant perspectives on children's exposure to such media culture. In the 1950s, some scholars described popular culture as "cancerous" (MacDonald, 1957), aligning it with the denigrative status of "Kitsch," which positions it as less than what is commonly viewed as "high" art and culture. Thinking critically about children and popular culture, Mitchell and Reid-Walsh (2002) provide some rather useful insights:

> Popular culture, especially mass-media culture, is often constructed as a monolithic giant, while the child is depicted as a powerless object who is about to be consumed. The researchers see themselves as off-screen saviors, rushing in to save the child who is unable to save himself or herself. The researchers, battling and conquering evil, play the role of the prince in fairy tales.
>
> (p. 2)

In reality, it is not only the researchers voluntarily playing the role of saviors, rescuing children from popular culture monsters, but also educators and parents who suddenly reduce children's ability to passive consumers when exposed to seemingly provocative contents. Indeed, this policing is quite precisely one of the many versions of the distribution of the sensible that positions children as lacking capability to discern qualities in media contents.

Calling popular culture that children consume kitsch, cancerous, or monstrous merely degrades children's ability of discretion as well as personal tastes and values. This seems to derive from a broader idea of the deficit child model, or the pre-sociological child images (James et al., 1998), that view children as, for example, inherently innocent, in a blank slate, or unconscious. It is a broader discourse, in which these Western ideologies of child development perpetuate the tendency to dominate every corner of children's lives. Anthropologist Ruth Benedict (1955) disrupts the normativity of Western ideas by suggesting that:

> From a comparative point of view, our culture goes to great extremes in emphasizing contrasts between the child and the adult. The child is sexless, the adult estimates his virility by his sexual activities; the child must be protected from the ugly facts of life, the adult must meet them without

psychic catastrophe; the child must obey, the adult must command this obedience: These are all dogmas of our culture, dogmas which, in spite of the facts of nature, other cultures commonly do not share.

(pp. 21–22)

These dogmas of our culture, to "protect" the innocent child in preservation of their uncontaminated nature, are what fuel the police of the distribution of the sensible. It restricts the being (e.g., citizenship) and doing (e.g., social activities) of young people, thus pushing them into marginalized partitions. This is not to suggest that all popular media is useful or that we should allow children to be exposed to any type of popular cultural contents. Rather, it is a critique of the adults' presumption that children are powerless and noncritical consumers, without attending carefully to the ways in which children encounter, consume, and reinterpret such cultural content.

What is important, though, is that children are very much aware of the restrictions placed on their consumption of popular visual culture. Perhaps because the policing of this process is so evident that they often use popular culture as a means to create their own sub cultures, which run counter to those of adults. Recently, sociologists and educational scholars have viewed children's popular cultural practices as an active process of meaning-making through daily peer interactions and the engagement in such popular cultural contents (Corsaro, 2015; James et al., 1998; Kleinfeld, 2001; Yoon, 2018). Specifically, James (1998) suggests that children define themselves as members of a culture of their own, in part because of the ways children work, think, and live "out of the lines" the adults have drawn for them:

> By confusing the adult order children create for themselves considerable room for movement within the limits imposed upon them by adult society. This deflection of adult perception is crucial for both the maintenance of continuation of the child's culture and for the growth of the concept of self for the individual child.
>
> (p. 395)

James's assertion suggests that children deliberately subvert adults' policing to make room for dissensual movements, which defines what they should appreciate or consume not only occurs commonly, but also serves as a crucial factor in continuing children's own culture. This deflection materializes in diverse forms, as children's culture is constituted by "all of the rules, norms, practices and things children make, do and use, as well as things made for them or sometimes even about them or around them" (Galman, 2019, p. 17). It is the visible and invisible materials, human bodies, and even the personal, social, and cultural ghosts that surround children's lives and their generational position, which varies greatly on the basis of their cultural context. Viewing everyday practices as a potential form of resistance, Michel de Certeau (1984) theorizes that a "nobody"—or, in Rancièrian terms, those with "no parts"—is capable of becoming a producer through the everyday practices of life rather than being the ordinary, passive consumer, and hence, of reconfiguring a given order. According to de Certeau, these everyday practices of consumption entail reading, writing, or consuming various products (e.g., stories, legends, newspapers, and articles of the dominant order), which has potential for consumers to become "the unrecognized producers, poets of their own acts, silent discoverers of their own paths" thus constituting "wandering lines ... in the jungle of functionalist rationality" (de Certeau, 1984, p. xviii). It is these lines of inflection, distinct from the lines of police, that constructs a dissensual consumption and production of culture. In this sense, children's everyday activities of reading, writing, drawing, and even the seemingly casual talking about popular media culture could function as a site of resistance.

Concerning how children's resistance manifests in artistic practices, Christine Thompson's (2003, 2006) observation of the "ket aesthetic" (see also James, 1998) provides a useful example. Ket aesthetics depicts young children's consumption of popular culture that often "prevails whenever a slackening of adult control occurs" (Thompson, 2006, p. 71). For children, in contrast to the adults' view, consuming this cultural content helps to assert their membership in a generational group that is distinct from other age groups, namely adults. In fact, the media culture images that children choose "provide a common language, pervasive evidence of one's place in the world, and potent motivations of drawing" (Thompson, 2003, p. 143). Consuming these popular cultural images often disapproved by adults, perhaps, is part of disrupting the distribution of social parts, emerging to formulate a sense of "we" (Rancière, 2015) as a collective demonstration.

My visits to the kindergarten classroom allowed opportunities to observe "ket aesthetics" happening in childhood spaces. When invited to participate in drawing popular culture figures, I disclosed my limited knowledge of even the longest-standing films and TV shows (e.g., Star Wars and Pokémon), as well as the vast and varied forms of contemporary media culture children consume today (e.g., PAW Patrol, Vampirina, Super Wings, etc.). Requesting a drawing, for example, children were quick to demonstrate in great detail the distinctive features and strengths of the characters so that I could learn about and utilize this information in the drawing process. Moreover, rather than a mere replication of preexisting images, the children reconfigured particular stories and scenes that were different from the original image references. At times, this required that I search Google images on my phone for photographic reference. However, I also wished to explore how art experiences might eventuate differently when unaccompanied by such technology. In consideration of this, I often suggested to the children that I draw without photo references, to rely on children's visual memories and narratives. In doing so, children partook in the work of drawing by directing me, completing my sketch, or coloring in the outlines I drew. Though unfamiliar, attending to this media content allowed me to demonstrate to the children a certain degree of "ignorance" (Rancière, 1991) toward popular cultural content. The vignette below describes how drawing popular culture figures allowed me to think about relational ethics in researching with children.

Drawing with Alex

On a Friday afternoon, Alex comes to the art table and waits patiently for me to finish my drawing for Anna. Upon its completion, he asks, "Now can you get a picture on your phone of Darth Vader and Luke Skywalker?" Having drawn numerous Star Wars characters over the last five months, I confidently declare that I now know how to draw both of them without looking it up. Doubtful, Alex asks, "But can you draw the lightsabers *clinging* together?" In an attempt to reassure him, I say, "I can try." Though Alex's facial expression remained uncertain, his actions seemed to be giving me permission to draw: Alex quietly picked up two Crayola markers, gray and black. "This [grey marker] is for Luke Skywalker, and this [black marker] is for Darth Vader," he says. After a short pause, he asked, "Can you *please* look it up?" Because I wished to see whether I could draw from memory the image and his description, I suggested that if he dislikes my drawing, he and I can draw again by looking at an image. Without an explicit agreement in place, he begins to describe the scene along with step-by-step instructions: "First, draw Luke Skywalker putting his lightsaber up in the sky, then draw Darth Vader's lightsaber laying in against." My confidence immediately diminishes the moment I begin to draw: "So the lightsaber going this way?" Without answering my question, he asks, "Can you draw this line a little thicker?" To which I respond, "Yes." Noticing that the marker I used was dry, Alex quickly leans toward the marker box, saying, "I'll get a different one. After you're done with Luke Skywalker and Darth Vader, can you look up the dock where they are fighting, and then draw the dock under them?" I agreed. By the time the lightsabers were illustrated, Alex wishes to color the lightsabers before Darth Vader's body is drawn. He uses blue for Luke Skywalker's lightsaber, verbally emphasizing that it is *under*. I ask, "Oh … What's the difference between being under and being over?" Continuing to color in, he explains, "Umm, under, if his is under, they will be blue in the middle here, and [if over] they will be red in the middle." He proceeds to diligently fill in both lightsabers.

As Alex took a turn to draw, I was pulled by other children who also had drawing requests. Completing both blue and red lightsabers, Alex calls me to attention: "Now can you finish drawing?" He then reaches for a thin black marker and places it on the table closer to me, saying, "Thin marker." I ask, "Oh, you want me to use the thin markers?" Holding the gray marker close to himself, Alex responds, "Yeah, and you know, grey is only for Darth Vader's gloves, and the rest of him is black. I'll give this to you when it's time." Then, to reaffirm that I am doing the right thing, he says, "You're drawing Darth Vader." As I am illustrating with the given marker, I ask, "Do you think his arm can come out from his cape?" He quickly responds, redirecting me: "No, his cape goes here." At this moment, the teacher calls attention to the children who had used the block play area (Alex was one of the children called on to clean up). Before leaving the seat, he looks at me and asks, "Can you keep drawing?"

I proceeded to draw Darth Vader's arm and a part of his cape. Alex returns shortly thereafter and glances at the drawing. He then grabs a thicker black marker to apply additional lines on top of those I had previously drawn. After thickening the lines a bit, he attached the cap to the marker and placed it on the table, near me. Then, looking at me, he says sternly, "You can start drawing." I say, "Okay, what's this?" A short answer returns, "Darth Vader." Pointing at the line next to the arm, I ask, "I mean, this part, what did you draw?" But he only repeated, "Draw the rest of Darth Vader." I still wanted to know about the mark next to Darth Vader's arm: "Okay, so, is this part of the cape that you drew?" Alex pauses, and then, fixing his eyes on the paper, sighs. With patience, he then attempts an explanation, "No, that is … that is … now …." Instead of continuing his explanation, he takes the marker from my hand and swiftly draws a horizontal line on top of the previously thickened line. He gives the marker back to me with an instruction: "Draw something like the helmet, draw his helmet." I check, "Draw his helmet above this line?" "Yeah, above that line." Still seeking for a satisfactory approval, I ask, "Like this? Does that look like his helmet?" Alex responds, "Yeah, but then draw his face part." I continue to raise multiple questions: "Doesn't it look like this? This could be part of his cape, right? From here?" As his eyes trace my hand's movement, he finally confirms, "Um-hmm." As I asked more questions on the placement of feet and arms, Alex, without answering my questions, again takes the marker from my hand to illustrate as he wished. At this moment, the teacher calls him again to clean up the pieces he had missed previously. Before leaving the table, he gives

Figure 5 Alex coloring the blue lightsaber.

Figure 6 Alex makes sure I continue to draw while he is gone.

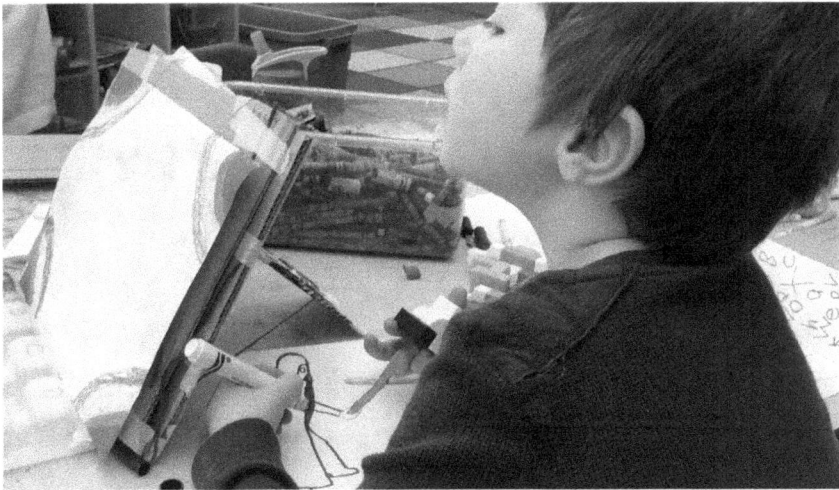

Figure 7 Alex listens to the teacher calling him again to clean up the blocks, hesitant to leave the seat. Shortly after, he says, "How could I miss that!".

me an assignment: "Can you make these lines as thick as this?" (see Figure 8). I continue to draw during his absence. He comes back in seconds and grabs the thin gray marker to thicken the contours of Luke Skywalker. At this moment we were drawing together—I was working on the left side, adding lines to the figure of Darth Vader, and Alex on the right side of the page.

Figure 8 Alex directs me to thicken other lines like the pointed part.

Figure 9 Lastly, Alex insists that we need to search an image of the fighting dock.

I finished my part sooner. Alex quietly and carefully continues to draw by leaning close toward the table, often backing up to see the whole picture. After doing so, he looks at me and asks, "Can you look up the dock Darth Vader and Luke Skywalker is fighting?" I inquire how it looks like, and he asserts, "No, you have to type it in. Cause' I don't know how it looks like."

Acknowledging that we both needed a reference to continue drawing, I open the Google application on my iPhone to search for the fighting scene Alex described. With the help of the photo reference, we completed the drawing by adding the background dock to the fighting scene.

Relational Ethics in Researching with Children

In the kindergarten classroom, my role developed into that of an artist-in-residence, who, at the request of the children assisted in the creation of characters and content related to the children's popular media interests. Faithful to my role as an accessible drawing tool, I carried out most of the general figure drawings without technical difficulty. But when it came to drawing some of the more specialized content from children's contemporary media culture, my status among the children immediately regressed— my drawing required assistance in sketching the characters desired by the children. As a recognition of my sparse knowledge, drawing requests were often accompanied with detailed descriptions of the characters' unique features, or demands that I search for images on my phone, which could then be used to aid my drawing. The point being, that by drawing together, the relationship entailed both the exchange of demands and expertise, as I was reliant on the child's cultural knowledge to deliver my graphic skills and the child utilized my graphic skills while also demonstrating his mastery of a particular media culture for me.

On the one hand, attending to each other's needs involved various forms of questioning, degrees of approval, and practices of negotiation. On the other hand, the process of asking for and attending to such questions, of accepting and resisting approval, and of being in negotiation, demanded that each of us, in different ways, establish the will to *un-know* what it is we think we understand about who the other is, about how they work, and the reasons they have for doing so. While the desire to know was ostensibly set forth and communicated, the process of un-knowing, however, required that each of us foster the willingness to work against ourselves, against the ideas and attitudes that sustain how we see and think the other. When drawing popular culture figures together, the process often demanded that the child share with me certain understandings about the popular media culture that was in question—a step that was typically unnecessary when children engaged in drawing with peers. For me, the experience of drawing with Alex entailed having to relinquish the aesthetic principles and methods of drawing that were most familiar. In lieu of these comforts, I found myself having to attend to the subtle shifts and uncertainties that would emerge, changes that made drawing something I was not accustomed to.

In exploring the process of working against oneself to accommodate the other, I discuss "ignorance" in drawing with children, a conceptual and ethical orientation that is grounded in the work of Rancière. I reconsider the adult-child relationship, which often subscribes to a dominant asymmetrical structure, whereby the adult gets to assume a form of superiority over the child. Rather than making the suggestion to completely undo these hierarchical relations, I explore a relational ethics of ignorance that brings to the child's and adult's traditional roles in relationships of inquiry, different and unanticipated ethical relations, which enable the child, the adult, and the relationship to become otherwise.

Ethics of Ignorance, Equality, and "Out of the Lines"

As was described in the drawing event with Alex and other kindergarteners, children are the "knowledge holders, the permission granters, and the rule setters for adults" (Walsh, 1998, p. 57). This overturn, of the traditional roles that children and adults occupy in research relationships, closely aligns with Rancière's (1991) elaboration of "intellectual equality," where he argues that one must *assume* equality, as "a point of departure" instead of an endpoint, "a *presupposition* rather than a goal, a *practice* rather than a reward situated firmly in some distant future" (Ross, 1991, p. xix, original italics). Here, I focus on how these two aspects of equality—presupposition and practice— materialized in my engagements with Alex's production of drawing Star Wars characters.

First, the *presupposition* of equality does not entail achieving an identical peer-status between the adult and the child—insofar as age, physical maturity, and cognitive development remain as apparent differences—but rather aims to minimize these differences by enacting a willful *ignorance* toward the ways in which these statuses center the adult as more-than. In drawing with Alex, a permission to fully disclose my vulnerability was given to myself. On each mark being made, I revealed my dependency on Alex's guidance, and Alex, in turn, tolerated my unusual level of ignorance in media culture that was so familiar to him. My dependency and Alex's tolerance were only possible upon the will to learn through the popular-cultural art production. That is, similar to how *Télémaque* was used in Jacotot's case in *The Ignorant Schoolmaster* (Rancière, 1991), the drawing of a Star Wars scene served as a mediator, or what Rancière (2011) calls as the "third thing," to narrow the skills and cultural knowledge gap between Alex and I. While Alex brought with him a proficient expertise of Star Wars, I was able to offer my proficiency in graphic production, thanks to the rigorous technique-oriented art education at the art hagwon. Consider, for example, that in spite of the unsettling projection of whether the particular envisioned scene could be precisely illustrated, the child artist willingly took the risk to permit the adult, who knows virtually nothing about the context, to contribute to the production. And I, in spite of having only meager knowledge of Star Wars, proceeded to draw by assuming that I could learn from the child by attending carefully to his patient guidance. We were both knowledgeable of where we were coming from yet ignorant of where we were going.

Furthermore, the collaborative drawing of popular culture figures constituted a *practice* of intellectual equality on the basis of ignorance that both the Alex and myself operated. One might easily confuse ignorance with indifference, a detached and static attitude toward what is happening at the moment. However, Rancièrian ignorance invites one to think about equality "actively," as a method of *doing* equality instead of only having equality (May, 2008). It is a matter of what people do, instead of what they receive, particularly what they do that challenges the roles the social structure assigned to them. When Alex and I relinquished our usual logic of action, together we attended to and affirmed the presupposition of equality. Then, we were also *doing* this by an active process that involved a deliberate ignorance to the taken-for-granted identities as well as operating the will to accommodate each other in the production of popular-cultural drawing. I further describe this ethics of ignorance along with other ethical considerations in following sections of this chapter.

The kind of equality that was produced in drawing with Alex was a negotiated equality, the many potentials of ongoing, emergent negotiations. I have elaborated earlier that arguing for equality is by no means to suggest becoming completely equal beings, as no two bodies could ever be equal unless they are the same person. Rather, it is a commitment to see what might happen if we set equality as a premise, to see the effects that would emerge differently from not presupposing equality at the first place. As Tanke (2011) echoes Rancière's idea of equality, he writes:

> [Rancière] does not argue that humans are essentially equal, but that all attempts to justify inequality are incoherent. The reason is simple: in order for authority to be more than arbitrary force, it must inevitably give reasons. This process of supplying reasons undermines the claims advanced on behalf of inequality, for when it attempts to explain the hierarchies it would erect, inequality presupposes equality.
>
> (p. 56)

In other words, equality is an ethical orientation of activating ignorance, to highlight the incoherency of inequality thus explores what might be produced if one presupposes and practices equality.

Drawing Star Wars figures with Alex led me to know and un-know about children and their culture, and to proceed in spite of the dominant social order that often trivializes children's production and consumption of culture. I learned about children's shared cultural contexts by taking the role of a drawing companion, one who does not—or does not only—impose knowledge, but also listens to children's interests and expertise. Alex and I were able to produce something outside of our usual works and roles, what Wilson (2007) refers to as an "other than child/other than adult" (p. 11) visual cultural production. On the basis of our "will to will" (Rancière, 1991) relationship, an "out of the lines" collaborative drawing emerged.

The process of drawing with Alex also entailed what education scholar Bronwyn Davies (2014) elaborates as "emergent listening." Different from listening "as usual," emergent listening seeks for the "not-yet-known" to disrupt one's judgments and prejudices, attending to "letting go of the status quo and of the quotidian lives embedded in that status quo" (p. 28). If listening as usual aligns with Rancière's concept of explication—namely, the practice of repetitive knowledge reproduction without demanding any new thoughts to come about—emergent listening invokes "ignorance" that suspends one's ready-made knowledge to allow critical thinking and the will to unknow to be operated thus generates effects of emancipation. This method of listening suggests not only the adult to listen critically and curiously to children but also, to preserve ignorance to the already-known knowledge about children's consumption and production of popular culture. Ethics, by definition, is the operation of will to achieve our own beliefs, values, desires, and inclinations, and acknowledging the difference between the uncontrollable power coming from the outside (e.g., others' beliefs, cultural differences, etc.). It is the will to confront the inevitable cultural and personal differences between one another thus seek for the ways in which reduce the gap. Therefore, activating ignorance is a profound ethical commitment for producing a child-adult relationship of equality.

Rancière's approach to research provides a useful insight for thinking about the ethics of "out of the lines." More than writing or teaching, Rancière's primary interest was in research, especially the archival research of delving into the French working-class texts. This materializes into his book *The Nights of Labor* (1989), where he demolishes the causal hierarchy by treating the workers' texts as same as any other texts, a creation "to be studied in their texture and their performance and not as expressions" (Rancière, 2016, p. 29). Rather than viewing the texts as less-than expressions, he took the unconventional perspective to recognize and study them as literary performances. Additionally, in doing the archival research, Rancière (2016) strayed away from the dominant causal logic, as he asserts that the search for a cause is the search for a hierarchy that merely constructs a "plot" that generates a distribution of the sensible of "what is possible to perceive or think" (Rancière, 2016, p. 29). Whereas subscribing to causality, or composing a plot, aligns with the usual modes of researching, Rancière's approach attends to the ethics of "out of the lines," one that disrupts the normalized order only regarding those assigned as "writers" to produce valid literature works.

The ethics of ignorance, or what I call the ethics of "out of the lines," seems akin to what Lewis (2012) describes as Rancière's "ethic of trust," which becomes "a way of fostering the development of extended social bonds without the remainder of political dissent" (p. 125). The ethics of trust, in this sense, is grounded in the "*demos* (in its anonymity, strangeness, and multiplicity) to verify equality for itself" (Lewis, 2012, p. 121), rather than experts or teachers telling the "truth," or explicate, for those who are assigned to the partition of labor, as an alternative dimension based on the assumption of equality. Vastly different from the consensus politics of current society, trust is a form of ignorance, in which thinkers and workers, and teachers and students, come together in dissensus despite its incongruity, with curiosity (see Chapter 6) and the will to activate the hypothesis of equality. Lewis (2012) further describes the ethics of trust by referencing Rancière's summary of the interconnection of trust and equality in relation to teaching children to draw, where Rancière (1991) writes "We will thus trust in the child's will to imitate. But we are going to *verify* that will" (p. 65, as cited in Lewis, 2012, p. 125). The trust in one's intellectual ability, especially in those who are rarely viewed as valid writers or artists capable of producing legitimate creative work, potentiates democratic possibilities.

I believe this speaks to the relational ethics that educators, scholars, researchers, and any interested adult of children's art should consider: not to regard children's work as expressions that associates with descriptions such as immature, child-like, or not-yet-developed, but to take their process and product of art making as we would treat any other artwork. It is also the causality in children's art (e.g., developmental analysis) that we consider dissociating with, as establishing a common logic in children's art only reduces individuals to a mere sequence of scientific rationale. Though an instantaneous temptation to discover the ostensible cause and effects might arise, I argue that we attend to the particularities—the narratives, context, lived experiences, and the relationship with human and nonhuman materials—of children's art practices for a contextual, and personally meaningful research.

Ethics of Answerability and Response-ability

The aesthetico-ethnographic study in the kindergarten classroom not only allowed my outsider membership to move toward the insider culture, but also away from my childhood art experiences. Because the art education I underwent at the hagwon continuously informs my perspectives on others' art practices, drawing unfamiliar subjects with children required me to activate my own ignorance. It demanded a willingness to alleviate the haunting voices of what is "proper" art and art education. As a means to "respect" the ghosts (Dernikos et al., 2019), specifically the ghosts of my haunting childhood art education, I hereby attempt to linger with these lines and dots entangled with personal histories and beliefs to inquire whether it might offer ethical insight to researching with children. To begin unraveling these lines in an ethical manner, I turn to philosopher Mikhail Bakhtin's (1990) discussion of ethics, specifically on the human obligation of "answerability." Bakhtin's ethics of answerability underscores the unique demands of responsibility in everyday interaction and textual communication that individuals face as they respond to "Others," an essential function of understanding and being a Self—or being *I*—a position into which an ethical obligation to enter to the community dialogically is given. Bakhtin (1990) asserts:

> This ever-present excess of my seeing, knowing, and possessing in relation to any other human being is founded in the uniqueness and irreplaceability of my place in the world. For only I—the one-and-only I—occupy in a given set of circumstances this particular place at this particular time; all other human beings are situated outside me.
>
> (p. 23)

For Bakhtin, every human's divergent subject position is simultaneously fully unique and fully limited. Bakhtin's concept of dialogism lies on this paradoxical premise, where, in a dialogical moment, the locational self attends to modes of communication (e.g., agreement and/or disagreement) by going "out of the lines." It is the unique *self* that produces new meanings with the world of the Other, through the process of creating respective ethical postures toward one another. Bakhtin (1986) also considers that, in culture,

> outsideness is a most powerful factor in understanding … A meaning only reveals its depth once it has encountered another foreign meaning … We raise new questions for a foreign culture, ones that it did not raise for itself; we seek answers to our questions in it, the foreign culture responds to us by revealing to us its new aspects and new semantic depths.
>
> (p. 7)

Here, the "outsideness," a desire for difference, exists as "the first pre-requisites for creatively understanding another person or another culture and for being creatively understood by them" (Emerson, 1996, p. 110). To experience and to speak are activities that demand the self to be in *chorus* of others, as Bakhtin (1990) notes that *"in a chorus* I do not sing for myself; I am active only in relation to the other and I am passive in the other's relation to me" (p. 121, original emphasis). I find that the kindergarteners and myself operated in chorus, in an harmony where I was an active operator to the children yet, on my part, I was given the children's relation to me without the ability to control the responses. Being in chorus, in fact, requires one to set forth vulnerability, one that necessitates exposure to the other(s)' relation to the "I." But because the other's relation to the self is not something malleable it requires continuous singing, the back and forth of presenting the self toward the other and exposing the self's vulnerability as a pre-acceptance of whatever response to come. In my case, although I was visiting the classroom primarily as an observer without any intention to interfere with the natural occurrences in the space, my being was in relation to the children's community and how they were performing in relation my presence defined my speaking and acting. Similar to Corsaro's (2015) understanding of children living in between the "two worlds," the children attended to their everyday lives being in relation to the Others—the adults as well as their peers.

Children not only live in the two worlds of the adult and the child, but also between "the division of nature and culture" (Prout, 2011, p. 7). As mentioned earlier, it is this hybridity of children that engender discomfort to adults for its difficulty to control and fully grasp the phenomenon of childhood. In her book *Staying with the Trouble: Making Kin in the Chthulucene*, Donna Haraway (2016) urges us to continually question our responses and accountabilities, rather than taking them for granted, as well as remain curious about the ethical implications of our acts. Similar to Bakhtin's answerability, Haraway (2016) introduces the ethics of "response-ability" by demonstrating how string figure games (e.g., Cat's Cradle) are played. In order to play the game and reach for an end, partners must take turns to accept and relinquish responsibilities. Though Haraway's post-humanist ideas take other species, environment, and nonhuman beings into consideration, I find it insightful in understanding adult-child relationships, particularly the drawing companionship I had with children in drawing popular culture figures. We accepted our response-ability to fill in the gap of cultural knowledge and graphic skills between us in order to reach for the end product of a drawing. I must admit that being put in the position of response-ability entailed unsettling tensions, because it is much easier to be in complete control of anything that seems controllable. It was our equally endowed intelligences (Rancière, 1991) that enabled us to attend to the drawing companionship being ignorant to the definition of our statuses (e.g., adult and child) yet it was these differences that mattered and had driven the journey of drawing together, as "we are not all response-able in the same ways" (Haraway, 2016, p. 29).

The ethics of answerability and response-ability are not so much about verbal communication but more about a matter of offering our greatest presence. Attending to the subtle nuances and particularities within the relational interaction, it is maximizing our abilities in order to remain curious about the other. This resonates with the methodological practice of "being there" (Schulte, 2011; Thompson, 2009) that embodies not only the verbal and performative interaction with children, but also the often silent act of observation and documentation. The careful and deliberate act of listening, seeing, thinking, and *being there* operates through a willingness to activate ignorance in researching with children. As such, the ethics of ignorance, answerability, response-ability, being-there, and "out of the lines" demands our full *commitment,* rather than a suggestion of an optional quality, to view children as "responsive and responsible moral agents" (Juzwik, 2004).

Though I describe these concepts of ethics along with my experience and relational interaction with the kindergarten children, I am hesitant to say that my research function as an answer to any ethical questions that might arise in research concerning children's art. Rather, my intention is to raise *more* questions for educators, researchers, and interested adults to reconsider some taken-for-granted knowledges and practices in the work we do, and further contemplate on how we might venture "out of the lines" in our practices. With arms wide open, it is an invitation to take the journey of complicating and politicizing the often simplified notions about children's lives and works. As such, if one desires to research, draw, read, write, or engage in even seemingly quotidian activities with children, embracing these relational ethics may open up new ways of thinking *with* and about children, out of the lines of our habitual modes of being and doing.

Conclusion: Imagining Emancipatory Art Pedagogies

Thus far in this book I have been quite faithful to aligning my argument with Rancière's view on pedagogy, politics, and aesthetics, as his radical standpoint fosters productive discussion in my study in the politics of childhood art. While I commend the diverse topics and artistic modes Rancière writes about, I find it important to note that there is an area that could be further explored in Rancière's work, one that leaves out childhood art and its pedagogy as part of the picture. Admittedly, children's art has been seldom addressed by theorists and philosophers who cover similar grounds. John Dewey, for example, had little to say directly about child art but the profound implications of his writings for that topic were teased out by others hence contributed immensely to the field of art education. Likewise, Rancière's method in his writings is provocative and educative precisely in the sense that it leads the readers to connect their experiences with the implications, without recipes for direct application to specific disciplines. However, because Rancière presents a unique standpoint and points out, repeatedly, that art in the aesthetic regime of art is for anyone, anywhere, and anytime, it becomes essential to understand what the nonrestrictive word "any" entails. Thus far in his work, what constitutes the population of "any" seems limited to adult artists and adult spectators, in the adult-dominant world, without particular consideration given to young children.

With this observation in mind, in this last chapter I first reflect on how my study furthers Rancière's work by raising the following questions: What happens when Rancière leaves out children's art in the discussion of the aesthetic regime of art, one that is supposed to be democratically inviting for anyone, anywhere, and anytime? How might including children's art as paradigmatic of the emancipatory and democratic tendencies of modernist and postmodern art disrupt Rancière's own theory and narrative? In discussing these inquiries, I move toward a critical appraisal of Rancière's work in light of childhood studies from being an application of his theories in order to open this book up to those outside the field of art education, especially Rancièrian scholars. Then, I discuss the ways in which to attend to a better police order, primarily drawing from Tyson Lewis's concept of "curiosity," and close this book by opening up a discussion on how curiosity could be at the center of our practices that moves toward emancipatory art pedagogies.

Art for Anyone, Anywhere, and Anytime?

Rancière has presented his long-standing interest in the arts, not only in visual arts but also in music, literature, film, theater, and other forms of creative modes throughout his work. In his conceptualization of the aesthetic regime of art, art involves much more than just a work of art, or even art as a whole in that "the aesthetic mode of thought is much more than a way of thinking about art. It is an idea of thought, linked to an idea of the distribution of the sensible" (Rancière, 2013b, p. 42). Art, in this sense, acts as an essential impetus for the working of this aesthetic mode of thought that is linked to a very specific form of political efficacy that Rancière calls emancipation—one is free from modes of representation and therefore "everyone and anyone is now entitled to intervene in any form of discourse, use or be addressed by any language and be the subject of representation" (Corcoran, 2015, p. 23). Art of the aesthetic regime presents a discontinuity with the assigned order of things that were part of the representational regime of art thus "offers resistance" to hierarchical orders and "embodies equality" (Lewis, 2016b, p. 551). In other words, equality is at the core of the aesthetic regime of art and therefore makes it political. Art is no longer submissive to the hierarchy of subjects and of publics and creates a disorder to the established partitions of who commissions the work, who creates it, and who gets to see it.

Despite this democratic view of aesthetic art, some critique Rancière's not-so-holistic view of art as his focus has been largely on the reception of the art rather than art production when it comes to the politics of art (see Lampert,

2017). I surmise that this asymmetric view of art is one of the reasons that account for childhood art being out of the picture of Rancière's thoughts. In *The Emancipated Spectator*, Rancière (2009a) presents a view that blurs the pronounced dichotomy between active artist and passive spectators—those who act and those who look. Rancière refers to this binary structure as the pedagogical model that is unequivocally hierarchical of power relations and inherently divisive, and that this underlying inequality between the knowledgeable artist and the ignorant spectator ought to be disrupted. Yet the determination of whether the inequality has been challenged is solely on the spectator's experience. That is, in order for the arts to be political, the consumer of the arts has to be affected and given a different experience. In this regard, the meaning of art that is in the aesthetic regime seems far too contingent on its social presentation, that demands that there be reception and appropriation of art, overlooking possibilities of art production being ontologically political.

In addition, Rancière presents a rather inconsistent view of who can be legitimate artists in the aesthetic regime of art. In *Aisthesis: Scenes from the Aesthetic Regime of Art* (2013b), a book that Rancière attempts to provide an empirical understanding of the aesthetic regime of art, the referred works Rancière elects to use as expletory forms of art are created by highly recognized European artists (e.g., Stéphane Mallarmé poems, Charlie Chaplin films). These are artists who can rightfully claim that they *are* professional artists, not those who produce art *despite* their "no part" status in the society. I find this particularly ironic given his dedication to argue in *The Nights of Labor* (1989) that the nineteenth-century proletarians' literary work done at night demands equality thus attempts to deconstruct the conventional categories of worker and thinker. The failure to consider politics of art in the process and production of art only deepens the binary between those who are artists and nonartists, as well as those who make art and receive art. Even when Rancière does present a seemingly democratic and comprehensive view of contemporary art, in relation to the redistribution of roles and capacities, it is not so much inclusive. He notes:

> we must not limit the precincts of art to galleries, museums, and fairs, which
> are only the most visible venues: There are also art schools, which train both

the favored artists of tomorrow and the activists of altermondialism; there
are forums for the discussion and presentation of work, research projects
and fieldwork financed by various institutions; there are activist artists
who live in squats, actors who work as social educators, parallel circuits of
musicians, video makers, and Internet artists developing all over the place.

(Carnevale & Kelsey, 2007, para. 14)

Though age is not mentioned in this range of artists, the types of work and
capacities depicted above seem remote from what child artists have access to
in daily life; they are sites and roles that adults primarily occupy and profess
on. In this sense, it is quite clear that children's art is hardly characteristic of the
arts that are emancipatory and political in Rancière's work.

Another observation I make to better understand why childhood art has yet
to have a place in Rancière's thoughts is that his words imply a subscription to a
particular image of a child and children. In *The Ignorant Schoolmaster* (1991),
Rancière depicts a figure of child and learning in his work but seems akin to
Rousseau's figure of child in *Emile* (see Chapter 2), of natural psychological
and intellectual development, but this could also mean that he is considering
a child to *become* political beings. What makes Rancière's differentiated, if not
discriminatory, position toward children clear is in the statement where he
writes about universal teaching (the method of Jacotot): "it is a question of
philosophy and humanity, not of recipes for children's pedagogy" (Rancière,
1991, p. 41). Children's pedagogy, here, is explicitly eliminated from the
imperative discussion of universal teaching for intellectual equality, in which
there is no inferior or superior minds, and conveniently considered less-than
important to be part of the question of philosophy and humanity that Rancière
painstakingly writes about. The fact that he uses the word "recipes," too,
insinuates that Rancière's view of children's pedagogy is rather a prescribed
formula than a divergent relational matter. This uneven standpoint of Rancière
is incongruous with his own elaboration of intellectual equality as well as the
art in the aesthetic regime as it itself creates partitions of who can possibly
learn or create art as legitimate beings.

Here I return to the question on how including children's art as paradigmatic
of the emancipatory and democratic tendencies of modernist and postmodern
art might disrupt Rancière's own theory and narrative. Acknowledging the gap

and intentionally including children's art into Rancièrian discussion re-orients Rancièrian thinkers to consider what really is democratic in art. Consistent with his idea of education where there is no longer relations of inequality between intelligences, therefore anyone can teach anyone anything anywhere and anytime, the Rancièrian notion of aesthetic equality suggests art residing in democracy, one that is on the basis of societal and political dissensus. When Rancière (2004b) formulates the aesthetics-art in that "art is art insofar as it is also non-art, or something other than art" (p. 36), he is thinking of the free play or tension between *poiesis* and *aisthesis* that involves "heterogeneous logics" (p. 46). Maintaining this tension is what Rancière sees as politics because it disrupts the police order and whatever breaks the configuration of parties governed by distribution of the sensible is politics (Rancière, 1999). As such, because children have long been minorities of the societies, their dissensual acts in art making, the intervention to the distribution of the sensible, most certainly falls into the definition of the aesthetics. Overlooking children as artists equally capable to make rupture into existing ideas of who gets to speak, create, view, and act within this regime, goes against the essence of politics.

Paradoxically, the minorities' artistic endeavor is precisely what Rancière studies in *The Nights of Labor* (1989), where proletarians' literary works are considered as legitimate forms of art. In it, Rancière depicts the workers' desire to cross the borders of prescribed conditions, which was virtually unimaginable during the time period. The deconstruction of the conventional partitions of worker and thinker, between those who are in perpetual manual labor and given to the work of thinking, troubled the bourgeois sensibilities. The workers were more-than workers, that of worker-poets or worker-musicians, who dared to break the boundary between the workers and thinkers by still doing labor during the day yet engaging in creative work during the night. Against all odds, they are now legitimate artists through their aesthetic mode of thought and therefore verified that all are equally intelligent. This is what Rancière calls political, a break from their given identity and enact as the other.

If the previously oppressed group of people can subvert their less-than identity and be legitimate artists, child artists should not be excluded from the image of artists as well. Bingham and Biesta (2010) argues that Rancière's figure of child is actually "already political" even before going to school in which they learn how to be autonomous (p. 57). They find that the figure of the child speaking, using verbal language, is no different from the figure of the (adult) person who engages in what Rancière calls politics, therefore a child learning language is not so much psychological but "rather a political account"—it requires one to "insert oneself into a distribution of the sensible where previously speech had not existed" (p. 59). The learning of visual language operates comparably to the learning of verbal language; one not only experiments with artistic elements, like babbling, but also discovers the right to be counted as a drawer or painter thus insert oneself to the existing distribution of the sensible of art. In other words, childhood art is already political. With this in mind, here I offer an encouragement to Rancièrian scholars that we stray away from compartmentalizing what we elect to include children and what not to, the very act that we are quick to criticize, as children using language is already political.

Further, for Rancière, aesthetic art is democratic not only because it is addressed by everyone and anyone, but also because anything and anyone can be its theme. Whereas art in the representational regime only depicts religious events, significant objects, or royal people, aesthetic art might put a urinal or commercial soup cans at the center of the work. Aesthetic art, in this sense, is democratic and political for its act of presenting anything and anyone as art, without any underlying code of appropriate subjects. Children, as seen in previous chapters, are not so restrictive on the themes and narratives that could be part of their art work. From objects they cherish in daily life to figures they see in media, anything become subjects of children's art practices. This is why I see children's art as inherently political: children have been demonstrating the potential to be political subjects and create art that reside in the aesthetic regime, regardless of adults' inability to notice them.

Now, if we are to actively consider children as artists and childhood art pedagogy as a legitimate one, what might our practices in the art classroom, or any other spaces, look like? As paradigmatic of the emancipatory and democratic tendencies of modernist and postmodern art, including children's art and its milieu of perceptions, narratives, events, and spaces itself *is* aesthetic. It is the politics I feel obligated to engage in as a researcher and interested adult in childhood art. The following sections focus on the pedagogical concerns of emancipation more broadly, which could be translated in other areas outside of art education.

Imagining Emancipatory Art Pedagogies:
A Better Police and Curiosity

If children are autonomous and political beings capable of creating art as legitimate artists, what is the need of educators in the classroom? Indeed, children benefit from the adults' guidance that scaffolds their learning, considering their relatively limited experience. One might ask that, along with this practical need, what is the pedagogical importance that is translated by the educator and what does such pedagogy look like? One might also assume that a student-centered education is more desirable than teacher-led, explicatory methods. In fact, student-centeredness has been a universal education trend, as seen in Reggio Emilia's philosophy, for example. However, Rancière's concept of education is neither teacher-centered (as this would be stultifying) nor student-centered (as the teacher still holds the authority to facilitate the learning) but attuned to the subject matter that move both the teacher and students toward democratic learning. This is seen in Jacotot's case where the material of *Télémaque* connected the teacher and the students to activate their equally endowed intellectual capacities thus lead to an emancipatory learning—the literature enacted as the "third thing" (Rancière, 2011).

By definition, art education is always concerned with the subject matter of art, and materials to engage with the ideas of art—objects, images, space, humans, etc. The teacher uses their intelligence and language to transfer their understanding of art, and the students, too, use the same intelligence to connect with such matters. Art as the *third thing* connects the bodies and therefore create avenues of learning and new experiences. Joris Vlieghe (2018) argues that Rancière provides us with a "thing centered" pedagogy that displaces both student- and teacher-centered forms; by focusing on the "thing" (the subject matter or materials such as books, drawings, songs, etc.), both the teacher and student demonstrate the equality of intelligence alongside each other thus practice the "real act of emancipation" (p. 925). In this sense, all art educators hold significant role to participate in emancipatory pedagogies that engage with students, materials, and matters, whether that being human or nonhuman.

To talk about emancipatory pedagogies, we have to remember the core premise of emancipation: the police order. Rancière (1999) maintains neutrality against the idea of a police order, stating that some police order is inevitable and one cannot exist in a purely free realm outside of a police order. Yet this acknowledgment that some police order is unavoidable is "neither to abandon a critical position on the police nor to reduce all police orders to the same level" (Deranty, 2014, p. 62). Moreover, while there could be "no pure 'outside' of the police order, this does not mean that the 'inside' of all police orders is equivalent" (Deranty, 2014, p. 62). In the study and practice of childhood art, too, it is no secret that dominant police orders (i.e., developmental paradigms, Western discourses of aesthetics and art practice) will continue to exist as long as children continue to make art. Rancière refuses to grant a normative preference to politics over police and I, too, am not suggesting that the study and educational practice of childhood art ought to or can be completely free of any given police order and always be political—again, as Rancière (1999) says, politics "happen very little or rarely" (p. 17). But what do we do with police that might be haunting us to a certain extent? While acknowledging its effects of existence, I believe it is generative to discuss how a healthy coexistence between police and political subjects as the police's nature being always on the opposite site of politics will remain the same.

Although there is no indication as to how a specific a police order could be assessed, Rancière (1999) states that not all police orders are the same and there is a "worse and a better police" (p. 31). Of course, a better police is not so much about the generosity nor better controllability of the police order. However, though he does comment on a better police being "the one that all the breaking and entering perpetrated by egalitarian logic has most often jolted out of its 'natural' logic" (p. 31), Rancière provides little definition on what makes a police more or less desirable. In imagining emancipatory art pedagogies that is entangled and emerges within this police order, I am compelled to further speculate what a more desirable police in might look like in the realm of childhood art education.

I find that Tyson Lewis's (2012, 2016b) discussion on "curiosity" offers generative ideas and help us better define Rancière's (1999) rather ambiguous concept of "a better police." Lewis (2012) observes that, though Rancière's educational reflection effectively suggests the radical change from intelligence to will, he misses to see how curiosity in his aesthetic redistribution of the sensible fits into his thinking. One might think of curiosity simply as a personal interest or feeling, or the age-old desire to *know*. Referring to Rancièrian idea of aesthetic, Lewis insists of curiosity more than this desire, being first and foremost located on the register of aesthetic and affected by the "aesthetic force which poses a certain challenge to the will" (2012, p. 87). The curious act begins from thinking and looking—a curious gaze therefore "reorients the field of the perceptible itself" (Lewis, 2016b, p. 558). It is a moment where we find ourselves in the "void," one that is not so much about lack but a "gap or fissure between (common or consensual) sense and (aesthetic) sense opened by a strange call" (Lewis, 2016b, p. 559). The aesthetics of curiosity, to paraphrase, is the urge to attend to the dissonance of senses yet maintaining ignorance to the endpoint of what that journey might entail. It is attending to the not-yet-seen, not-yet-heard, or the experiences that are yet to be had, which can be observed in children's art practices. Consider Oliver and Brian's case (see Chapter 4), where the children took the route to explore what painting big dots out of the assigned lines would produce, as a rupture of making sense or demonstrating what they were supposed to do. Furthermore, curiosity is a fall for its embodied unintentionality (Lewis, 2016b, p. 559). In their exodus, Oliver and Brian were actively availing themselves to ignorance, particularly the indifference toward the consequences of their performances. One might describe this as getting lost or rebellious. This is in fact precisely what curiosity is, as a curious mind does not seek easy, one-right answers, but seeks to move toward the unknown and the uncanny. Curiosity, thus, produces pedagogical, aesthetic, and political affects, "blur[ring] the false obviousness of strategic schemata" (Rancière, 2009a, p. 104).

In thinking about how curiosity could be seen as one of the characteristics of a better police, and therefore attend to emancipatory pedagogies, I wonder if this notion of curiosity could be expanded to the pedagogical community. Lewis's note on the aesthetics of curiosity already implies that we attend to the inconsistency of senses but remain ignorant to the result of the journey. As the children's political acts seen in Chapter 4 also depict an explicitly communal engagement, I argue here that the aesthetics of curiosity in emancipatory pedagogies can occur as a community. In fact, political philosopher Perry Zurn (2021) characterizes curiosity not only as the desire, impulse, feeling to fill in the gap, understand, or gain information about things, but also as "a distinguishing mark of resilience and coalition building within those same marginalized communities" (Zurn, 2021, p. 3). In other words, beyond an individual level, curiosity can be a communal act, to an extent that it could be a political and construct political communities. Moreover, curiosity can be seen as a

> social praxis tuned to specific political formations. Curiosity is a series of investigative practices that are informed by and constructive of political architectures. For me, curiosity is less what one person feels than what one or more persons do, always within existing and shifting sociopolitical contours.
>
> (Zurn, 2021, p. 12)

In this sense, curiosity is heavily contingent upon the relational, social, political matters. And, importantly, curious mind(s) can cultivate and enact their questions beyond the given distribution of the sensible, an extent to which it disrupts established patterns of knowledge or institution. In *The Ignorant Schoolmaster*, Rancière describes an emancipated community as "a society of artists," which:

> would repudiate the division between those who know and those who don't, between those who possess or don't possess the property of intelligence. It would only know minds in action: people who do, who speak about what they are doing, and who thus transform all their works into ways of demonstrating the humanity that is in them as in everyone.
>
> (p. 71)

This holds promise of a new world of art and a new life for curious individuals and communities: the aesthetic experience eludes the distribution of roles and competences which structures the hierarchical order. These are powerful experiences in the sense that make one think, interpret, and feel beyond the certainty of facts.

Returning to Rancière's idea of a better police, I speculate that a police order that leaves gaps to explore and intensify one's curious mind could potentially be a better police. This could also entail being more of an inclusive police, where politics emerge to render instances of democratic education, for instance. In education, the institution of school and explanatory methods will always exist as police order, as learning cannot be fully free from such long-preserved establishments. In fact, Rancière's intent in *The Ignorant*

Schoolmaster is not to abolish all structures like schools or schoolmasters nor create an opposition between teaching and learning (teaching always being authoritarian, explanatory, and bad, and learning as agentic, emancipatory, and good). Explication is actually not always bad: Bingham and Biesta (2010) assert that explanation only becomes a problem "when it is constructed as a vehicle for emancipation," "taken for a metaphor as to how society is supposed to operate," and "assumed to explain how people actually learn things" (p. 154). At other occasions, like police, explication can happen in various ways yet not so much that it serves as a direct path to emancipation.

Perhaps we can call this "a better explication." In the discourse of childhood art, finding void within the artistic and pedagogical theories and practices that are upheld as "truth" could be one approach to see the police order as better, as well as to encourage political subjects to fall into curiosity. Because police orders may make more or less space for the emergence of politics (Rancière, 2006c), to utilize that potential space for democratic politics is contingent on our will. Curiosity can also be connected with the ethics of "out of the lines" and the "ethics of trust" (Lewis, 2012) mentioned in Chapter 5, as defining features of what I call the art of being better police. That is, grounded in the supposition of intellectual equality between the teacher and students, the ethics of trust could maximize one's curiosity and open up possibilities of the police to be better. What becomes important is not to consider explication as a tool to reach for emancipation or, conversely, emancipation as something that can be reached. Rather, what a better police allows us to think about is to be practically curious and begin from a completely different starting point of assuming all intelligences as equal. This, in short, is emancipation.

In this book, I have described three main pedagogical events that are quite distinct in its nature where different kinds of art pedagogies multiply and move through various combinations of expertise, authority, and, ultimately, curiosity. The opening scene of Ms. Lee's harsh instructions in the cabbage drawing event and me being spanked by her for not meeting expectations alludes to the pedagogy of "bad police." The teacher had both authority and expertise, and students were not allowed to perform outside of assigned rules. Then, Ms. Carla in Chapter 4 could be seen as someone who has expertise but chooses not to exert authority. Though she did demonstrate rules to follow in the prompted painting activity, she did not reprimand Oliver and

Brian for painting out of the lines, although she certainly could have. It could be assumed that curiosity is somewhat present in this case, but not in an apparent way. Finally, the event of my drawing Star Wars figures with Alex in Chapter 5 could be described as "curious" teaching for I, the adult, had neither expertise nor authority. Rather, Alex, the child, had considerably more expertise on the content and taught *me* how to draw. This perhaps aligns with the idea of "better police," as opposed to Ms. Lee's policing in the art hagwon. In comparing and contrasting these events, I am reminded of Rancière's point on activating one's will. The teacher's authority or expertise is not so much an essential precondition for meaningful art teaching and learning, but the will to relinquish what one already knows and be curious about the other. Even if one does not exactly replicate the method of "the ignorant schoolmaster" as described by Rancière, emancipatory pedagogy can be imagined in any teacher-student relationship with diverse expertise, maximizing its unique circumstances.

In closing, it is my hope to have added to Rancière's wide range of narratives in arts and pedagogy through this book, in that childhood art is aptly described as one kind of politics in imagining democratic and emancipatory pedagogies. For anyone entering or continuing the pedagogical work, it is important to note that we weave in the relational, political, and ethical matters in the "problematic of co-existence" (Atkinson, 2018, p. 211). As emancipation is "entirely practical" (Bingham & Biesta, 2010, p. 155), it is important to imagine emancipatory pedagogies beyond theories and ponder how our assumptions and acts could be practically manifested. As Rancière (1991) notes, "it's not a matter of making great painters; it's a matter of making the emancipated: people capable of saying, 'me too, I'm a painter'" (p. 67).

Notes

Introduction

1   In South Korea, 6th grade is the last grade of elementary school (elementary: 1st–6th grade, middle school: 7th–9th grade, high school: 10–12th grade).

Chapter 1

1   See Chapter 2 for more discussion on images of the child.
2   Online Etymology Dictionary (https://www.etymonline.com/word/emancipate)
3   According to Rockhill (2013), a wrong is "a specific form of equality the establishes the 'only universal' of politics as a polemical point of struggle by relating the manifestations of political subjects to the police order … A wrong can only be treated by modes of political subjectivization that reconfigure the field of experience" (p. 98).
4   Rancière's term *La Subjectivation* could be translated as "subjectification," "subjectivation," or "subjectivization" (see Rancière, 2013a, p. 97).
5   In *Republic,* Plato excluded both democracy and theater in order to construct an ethical community, a community of organic life without politics. Both art and politics were excluded, thus the artisan held no power to engage in free play besides the true or false imitations.

Chapter 2

1   Whereas "revenant" means the ghost, "a coming back" or "return," the arrivant is a guest or a newcomer, which is always "to come" in the future. When the arrivant haunts, it indicates the coming of a past that calls for a more just future (Derrida, 1994).

2   Plato's words are *eidos* and *idea* in Greek. This is different from the modern English definition of "idea," for Plato's Forms are not mental entities, but rather "subject of independent truths, not reducible to or dependent on facts about its sensible manifestations" (Sedley, 2016, p. 11). In other words, Forms are independently existing entities only graspable by the mind, though they are not dependent on being grasped in order to exist.

3   In *Discipline and Punish*, Foucault (1975) demonstrated how a regulatory gaze and constant surveillance that are often subtle and thereby seemingly invisible transformed individuals into docile bodies leading to normalization and acceptance of systems.

4   In *The Ignorant Schoolmaster*, Rancière (1991) tells the story of Joseph Jacotot who believed that differences in performance derived from inability to attend rather than from innate intellectual differences and therefore all people were of equal intelligence. I further elaborate on Rancière's idea of intellectual equality in detail in the next chapter.

5   Though I describe the "Draw-a-Man" test as a completed study widely received in the twentieth century, it is important to note that there are a number of researches today that utilize this test as a method (e.g., Dey & Ghosh, 2016; Latorre-Román et al., 2016; Picard, 2015).

6   It is essential to note how the term "aesthetics" is used in this section. Though I will refer to a different definition of aesthetics in the next chapters (i.e., Rancière's definition of aesthetics), aesthetics here denotes a general understanding that broadly considers a theory of beauty, sensibility or taste, which is interchangeably used with style. Such notion of aesthetics therefore concerns the "visual appearance of effects" (Williams, 1976, p. 28) and/or a "sense perception" (Eagleton, 1990).

7   As art can be an outlet for intense feelings and a site for vast imagination, in most cases, I would argue against censoring images and stories that appear in young children's drawings. Suppressing particular types of expression only casts a shadow of fear thus leads to conformity and voluntary curtailment of expression. However, I also believe that educators hold vital responsibility to facilitate conversations when sexist, racist, and other harmful stereotypes enter the visual landscape of an art classroom. As a way to navigate the interest in both freeing up art from a long history of structures, and taking what children reveal more seriously (without policing its quality), I suggest that we engage in critical conversations that unpack the concerns with students and reorient them to other qualities and topics art can offer.

Chapter 3

1   See Chapter 1 on "subjectivization."
2   Although it is difficult to establish an ideal length of an ethnographic study, earlier anthropologists researching in rural cultures spent at least twelve-months in order to experience the annual cycle of the growing season (Jeffrey & Troman, 2004).
3   An emic perspective is understanding a culture as an insider point of view, focusing on the particularities and internal schemes, and an etic perspective is taking a general, nonstructural, and objective point of view. Namely, in the case of researching with children, as an empirical study by nature, an emic approach might incorporate the voice of children whereas an etic research would primarily use the voice of a researcher. However, it is important for the researcher to have both perspectives in ethnographic research. In the case of my research, it was essential for me to understand the insider culture and shared understandings in the kindergarten classroom, as well as to attain an etic perspective based on my emic standpoint in the fieldwork of ethnographic research.

Chapter 4

1   Here, I use plural to suggest that the adult power is not limited to Ms. Carla but also adults in general that constitutes the less-than image of childhood, which consequently put children to the partition of having no part.
2   Ware (1973) states that, while both acts and actions concern doings rather than happenings, the two concepts are different from one another not only for the common use of the expressions, but also for the six conditions.
3   In their book *A Thousand Plateaus: Capitalism and Schizophrenia* (1987), philosophers Gilles Deleuze and Felix Guattari compare "tracing" with the construction of maps, in which the former only generates fixed and predictable paths and the latter opens up possibilities of adaptation and reconstruction.

Chapter 5

1   This quote comes from Shakespeare's *Hamlet,* who is lamenting the appearance of his father's ghost. Derrida (1994) uses this phrase to describe the nonlinear and uncontaminated conception of time throughout *Specters of Marx.*

References

Adler, P. A., & Adler, P. (1987). *Membership roles in field research*. Newbury Park, CA: Sage Publications.

Alderson, P. (2008a). *Young children's rights: Exploring beliefs*. Philadelphia, PA: Jessica Kingsley Publishers.

Alderson, P. (2008b). Children as researchers: Participation rights and research methods. In P. Christensen & A. James (Eds), *Research with children* (2nd ed.). (pp. 276–290). London: Rutledge.

Archard, D. (1993). *Children: Rights and childhood*. London; New York: Routledge.

Ariès, P. (1965). *Centuries of childhood: A social history of family life*. New York: Vintage Books, Random House.

Aristotle, & Keyt, D. (1999). *Politics*. New York; Oxford: Clarendon Press.

Arnheim, R. (1974). *Art and visual perception: A psychology of the creative eye* (Expand and rev. ed.). Berkeley: University of California Press.

Atkinson, D. (2018). *Art, disobedience, and ethics: The adventure of pedagogy*. Cham, Switzerland: Palgrave Macmillan.

Bae-Dimitriadis, M. (2015). Performing "planned authenticity": Diasporic Korean girls' self-photographic play. *Studies in Art Education, 56*(4), 327–334.

Bath, C., & Karlsson, R. (2016). The ignored citizen: Young children's subjectivities in Swedish and English early childhood education settings. *Childhood, 23*(4), 554–565.

Bakhtin, M. M. (1990). *Art and answerability: Early philosophical essays* (V. Liapunov, & K. Brostrom, Trans.). Austin: University of Texas Press.

Bakhtin, M. M., & Holquist, J. M. (1986). *The dialogic imagination: Four essays*. Austin: University of Texas Press.

Balagopalan, S. (2014). *Inhabiting "childhood": Children, labor, and schooling in postcolonial India*. New York: Palgrave Macmillan.

Barad, K. (2012). "Matter feels, converses, suffers, desires, yearns and remembers": Interview with Karen Barad. In R. Dolphijn, & I. van der Tuin (Eds), *New materialism: Interviews & cartographies*. Open Humanities Press. An imprint of Michigan Publishing, University of Michigan Library.

Barblett, L., Knaus, M., & Barratt-Pugh, C. (2016). The pushes and pulls of pedagogy in the early years: Competing knowledges and the erosion of play-based learning.

Australasian Journal of Early Childhood, 41(4), 36–43. https://search.informit.org/doi/10.3316/informit.619041648336775.

Berger, P., & Luckmann, T. (1967). *The social construction of reality: A treatise in the sociology of knowledge* (1st ed.). Garden City, NY: Doubleday.

Benedict, R. (1934). *Patterns of culture.* New York: Harcourt Brace.

Benedict, R. (1955). Continuities and discontinuities in cultural conditioning. In M. Mead & M. Wolfenstein (Eds), *Childhood in contemporary cultures* (pp. 21–30). Chicago, IL: University of Chicago Press.

Bernstein, R. (2011). *Racial innocence: Performing American childhood from slavery to civil rights.* New York: New York University Press.

Biesta, G. (2008). Toward a new "logic" of emancipation: Foucault and Rancière. *Philosophy of Education Yearbook*, 169–177.

Biesta, G. (2011). The ignorant citizen: Mouffe, Rancière, and the subject of democratic education. *Studies in Philosophy and Education, 30*(2), 141–153.

Bingham, C., & Biesta, G. (2010). *Jacques Rancière: Education, truth, emancipation.* London; New York: Bloomsbury Academic.

Boas, F. (1974). Human faculty as determined by race. In G. W. Stocking (Ed.), *The shaping of American anthropology, 1883–1911: A Franz Boas reader* (pp. 221–242). New York: Basic Books (originally published 1894).

Bryan, N., & Jett, C. (2018). Playing school. *Journal for Multicultural Education, 12*(2), 99–110.

Burman, E. (2017). *Deconstructing developmental psychology* (3rd ed.). London: Routledge

Bühler, K. (1930). *The mental development of the child. A summary of modern psychological theory.* Oxford, England: Harcourt, Brace.

Cannella, G. S. (1997). *Deconstructing early childhood education: Social justice and revolution* (3rd ed.). New York: Peter Lang Inc.

Carnevale, F., & Kelsey, J. (2007). Art of the possible: An interview with Jacques Rancière. *Artforum*, March.

Castro, J. C. (2012). Learning and teaching art through social media. *Studies in Art Education, 53*(2), 152–169.

Castro, J. C., Lalonde, M., & Pariser, D. (2016). Understanding the (im)mobilities of engaging at-risk youth through art and mobile media. *Studies in Art Education, 57*(3), 238–251.

Chalmers, G. (1996). *Celebrating pluralism: Art, education, and cultural diversity.* Los Angeles, CA: Getty Center for Education in the Arts.

Christensen, P. H. (2004). Children's participation in ethnographic research: Issues of power and representation. *Children & Society, 18*, 165–176.

Citizen. (n.d.). In *Oxford English Dictionaries Online*. Retrieved from https://en.oxforddictionaries.com/definition/citizen.

Clark, A. (2003). The Mosaic approach and research with young children. In V. Lewis, M. Kellet, C. Robinson, S. Fruser, & S. Ding (Eds), *The reality of research with children and young people* (pp. 157–161). London: Sage Publications.

Clark, A., & Moss, P. (2001). *Listening to young children: The Mosaic approach*. London: National Children's Bureau for the Joseph Rowntree Foundation.

Clifford, J., & Marcus, G. E. (1986). *Writing culture: The poetics and politics of ethnography: A school of American research advanced seminar*. Berkeley: University of California Press.

Cockburn, T. (2013). *Rethinking children's citizenship*. New York: Palgrave Macmillan.

Cohen, E. F. (2005). Neither seen nor heard: Children's citizenship in contemporary democracies. *Citizenship Studies, 9*(2), 221–240

Cook-Gumperz, J., Corsaro, W. A., & Streeck, J. (1986). *Children's worlds and children's language*. Berlin, Germany: Walter de Gruyter.

Corcoran, S. (2015). Editor's introduction. In J. Ranciere, & S. Corcoran (Eds), *Dissensus: On politics and aesthetics* (pp. 1–24). London; New York: Continuum.

Cornwall, J., & Park, H. (2022). Leaking and containing: Researching with children and the sketchbook. *Qualitative Inquiry, 28*(8–9), 888–895. https://doi.org/10.1177/10778004221075247.

Caroline, P. (2009). Rancière and the poetics of the social sciences. *International Journal of Research & Method in Education, 32*(3), 267–284. DOI: 10.1080/17437270903259741.

Corsaro, W. A. (1985). *Friendship and peer culture in the early years*. Norwood, NJ: Ablex Pub. Corp.

Corsaro, W. A. (2003). *We're friends, right?: Inside kids' culture*. Washington, DC: Joseph Henry Press.

Corsaro, W. A. (2015). *The sociology of childhood* (4th ed.). Thousand Oaks, CA: Pine Forge Press.

Corsaro, W. A., & Eder, D. (1990). Children's peer cultures. *Annual Review of Sociology, 16*, 197–220.

Creswell, J. W., & Poth, C. N. (2018). *Qualitative inquiry & research design: Choosing among five approaches* (4th ed.). Thousand Oaks, CA: SAGE.

Cutler, D., & Frost, R. (2001). *Taking the initiative: Promoting young people's involvement in public decision-making in the UK*. London: Carnegie Young People Initiative.

Dahlberg, G., Moss, P., & Pence, A. R. (1999). *Beyond quality in early childhood education and care: Postmodern perspectives*. London; Philadelphia, PA: Falmer Press.

Davies, B. (2014). *Listening to children: Being and becoming* (1st ed.). London; New York: Routledge.

Davis, O. (2010). *Jacques Rancière*. Cambridge; Malden, MA: Polity.

De Certeau, M. (1984). *The practice of everyday life* (S. Rendall, Trans.). Berkeley: University of California Press.

Deleuze, G., & Guattari, F. (1987). *A thousand plateaus: Capitalism and schizophrenia*, (B. Massumi, Trans.). Minneapolis: University of Minnesota Press.

Denzin, N. K. (1989). *Interpretive Interactionism*. Newbury Park: Sage.

Deranty, J. (2014). *Jacques Rancière: Key concepts*. Abingdon, Oxon & New York, NY: Routledge. https://doi.org/10.4324/9781315711485.

Dernikos, B. P., Ferguson, D. E., & Siegel, M. (2019). The possibilities for "humanizing" posthumanist Inquiries: An intra-active conversation. *Cultural Studies ↔ Critical Methodologies*. https://doi.org/10.1177/1532708619829793.

Derrida, J. (1994). *Spectres of Marx*. New York: Routledge.

Dey, A., & Ghosh, P. (2016). Do human-figure drawings of children and adolescents mirror their cognitive style and self-esteem? *International Journal of Art and Design Education, 35*, 68–85.

Dobrowolsky, A. (2002). Rhetoric versus reality: The figure of the child and new labour's strategic "social investment state". *Studies in Political Economy, 69*(1), 43–73.

DuBois, C. (1944). *The people of Alor*. Minneapolis: University of Minnesota Press.

Duncum, P. (1982). The origins of self-expression: A case of self-deception. *Art Education, 35*(5), 32–35.

Duncum, P. (1987). What, even Dallas? Popular culture within the art curriculum. *Studies in Art Education, 29*(1), 6–16.

Duncum, P. (2009). Toward a playful pedagogy: Popular culture and the pleasures of transgression. *Studies in Art Education, 50*(3), 232–244.

Duncum, P. (2014). Revisioning premodern fine art as popular visual culture. *Studies in Art Education, 55*(3), 203–213.

Duncum, P. (2018). Drawing in art education research: A literature review. *Australian Art Education, 39*(2), 223–235.

Dyson, A. (1997). *What difference does difference make? Teacher reflections on diversity, literacy, and the urban primary school*. Urbana, IL: National Council of Teachers of English.

Dyson, A. H. (2003). *The brothers and sisters learn to write: Popular literacies in childhood and school cultures*. New York: Teachers College Press.

Dyson, A. H., & Genishi, C. (2005). *On the case: Approaches to language and literacy research*. New York: Teachers College Press.

Eagleton, T. (1990). *The ideology of the aesthetic*. Oxford: Basil Blackwell.

Efland, A. (1976). The school art style: A functional analysis. *Studies in Art Education, 7*(2), 37–44.

Efland, A. (2004). The entwined nature of the aesthetic: A discourse on visual culture. *Studies in Art Education, 45*(3), 234–251.

Eisner, E. (1978). NAEA commission report. In C. Dorn (Ed.), *Report of the NAEA commission on art education*. Reston, VA: National Art Education Association.

Eisner, E. (1988). Discipline-based art education: Its criticisms and its critics. *Art Education, 41*(6), 7–13. https://doi.org/10.1080/00043125.1988.11651412.

Emancipation. (n.d.). In *Online Etymology Dictionary*. Retrieved from https://www.etymonline.com/word/emancipate.

Emerson, C. (1996). Keeping the self intact during the culture wars: A centennial essay for Mikhail Bakhtin. *New Literary History, 27*(1), 107–126.

Emerson, R. M., Fretz, R. I., & Shaw, L. L. (2011). *Writing ethnographic fieldnotes* (2nd ed.). Chicago, IL: University of Chicago Press.

Faulks, K. (2000). *Citizenship*. London: Routledge.

Ferguson, A. A. (2001). *Bad boys: Public schools in the making of black masculinity*. Ann Arbor: University of Michigan Press.

Fine, G. A., & Glassner, B. (1979). Participant observation with children: Promise and problems. *Journal of Contemporary Ethnography, 8*(2), 153–174.

Fortes, M. (1949). *The web of kinship among the Tallensi*. Oxford: Oxford University Press.

Foucault, M. (1975). *Discipline and punish: The birth of the prison*. New York: Vintage Books.

Foucault, M. (1980). *Power /knowledge: Selected interviews & other writings 1972– 1977* (C. Gordon, Ed.). New York: Patheon Books.

Foucault, M. (1991). Questions of method. In G. Buechell, C. Gordon, & P. Miller (Eds), *The Foucault effect* (pp. 73–86). Chicago, IL: University of Chicago Press.

Freedman, K. (2003). *Teaching visual culture: Curriculum, aesthetics and the social Life of art*. New York, NY: Teachers College Press.

Freire, P. (2000). *Pedagogy of the oppressed* (30th anniversary ed.). New York: Continuum.

Gage, M. F. (2019). *Aesthetics equals politics: New discourses across art, architecture, and philosophy*. Cambridge, MA: MIT Press.

Galman, S. C. (2019). *Naptime at the O.K. corral: Shane's beginner's guide to childhood ethnography*. Abingdon, Oxon; New York: Routledge.

Gardner, H. (1980). *Artful scribbles: The significance of children's drawings*. New York: Basic Books.

Geertz, C. (1973). *The interpretation of cultures: Selected essays*. New York: Basic Books.

Genel, K. (2016). Jacques Rancière and Axel Honneth: Two critical approaches to the political. In K. Genel, & J. Deranty (Eds), *Recognition or disagreement: A critical encounter on the politics of freedom, equality, and identity* (pp. 3–32). New York: Columbia University Press.

Goodenough, F. L. (1926). *Measurement of intelligence by drawing*. New York: Harcourt, Brace, and World.

Gordon, A. (1997/2008). *Ghostly matters: Haunting and the sociological imagination*. Minneapolis: University of Minnesota Press.

Graue, M., & Walsh, D. (1998). *Studying children in context: Theories, methods, and ethics*. Thousand Oaks, CA: Sage Publications.

Greenberg, P. (1996). Time, money, and the new art education versus art and irrelevance. *Studies in Art Education, 37*(2), 115–116.

Guénoun, S., & Kavanagh, J. (2000). Jacques Rancière: Literature, politics, aesthetics: Approaches to democratic disagreement. *Sub-Stance* (92), 3–24.

Hallward, P. (2006). Staging equality: On Rancière's Theatrocracy. *New Left Review, 37* (January/February), 109–129.

Hallward, P. (2009). Staging equality: Rancière's theatrocracy and the limits of anarchic equality. In G. Rockhill, & P. Watts (Eds), *Jacques Rancière: History, politics, aesthetics* (pp. 140–157). Durham, NC: Duke University Press.

Haraway, D. J. (1991). *Simians, cyborgs and women: The reinvention of nature*. London: Free Association Books.

Haraway, D. J. (2016). *Staying with the trouble: Making kin in the Chthulucene*. Durham, NC: Duke University Press.

Harris, D. B. (1963/1991). *Goodenough-Harris drawing test: Manual*. San Antonio, TX: The Psychological Corporation & New York: Harcourt Brace Jovanovich.

Heitzenrater, R. (2001). John Wesley and children. In M. Bunge (Ed.), *The child in Christian thought* (pp. 279–299). Grand Rapids, MI: Eerdmans.

Henward, A. S. (2015). (Re)imagining participant observation with preschool children. In W. Parnell, & J. M. Iorio (Eds), *Disrupting early childhood education research: Imagining new possibilities* (pp. 73–85). New York: Routledge.

Hirschfeld, L. (2002). Why don't anthropologists like children? *American Anthropologist, 104*(2), 611–627.

Howard, J. (2021). Toy guns: Black mixed-race boys and the desire to play. *Taboo: The Journal of Culture and Education, 20*(1). Retrieved from https://digitalscholarship.unlv.edu/taboo/vol20/iss1/2.

Irwin, R., & de Cosson, A. (Eds). (2004). *A/r/tography: Rendering self through arts-based living inquiry.* Vancouver: Pacific Educational Press.

Isin, E. F. (2008). Theorizing acts of citizenship. In E. F. Isin, & G. M. Nielsen (Eds), *Acts of citizenship* (pp. 15–43). London: Palgrave Macmillan.

Isin, E. F., & Turner, B. S. (2002). Introduction. In E. F. Isin, & B. S. Turner (Eds), *Handbook of citizenship studies* (pp. 1–10). London: SAGE Publications.

Ivashkevich, O. (2009). Children's drawing as a sociocultural practice: Remaking gender and popular culture. *Studies in Art Education, 51*(1), 50–63.

Ivashkevich, O., & Shoppell, S. (2013). Appropriation, parody, gender play, and self-representation in preadolescents' digital video production. *International Journal of Education & the Arts, 14*(2).

James, A. (1998). Confections, concoctions, and conceptions. In H. Jenkins (Ed.), *The children's culture reader* (pp. 394–405). New York: New York University Press.

James, A. (2001). Ethnography in the study of children and childhood. In P. Atkinson, A. Coffey, S. Delamont, J. Lofland, & L. Lofland (Eds), *Handbook of ethnography* (pp. 246–257). London; Thousand Oaks, CA: SAGE Publications.

James, A. (2005). Life times: Children's perspectives on age, agency and memory across the life course. In: Qvortrup, J. (Eds), *Studies in modern childhood* (pp. 248–266). London: Palgrave Macmillan. https://doi.org/10.1057/9780230504929_15.

James, A. (2007). Giving voice to children's voices: Practices and problems, pitfalls and potentials. *American Anthropologist, 109*(2), 261–272.

James, A., & James, A. L. (2012). *Key concepts in childhood studies* (2nd ed.). Los Angeles, CA: Sage Publications Ltd.

James, A., Jenks, C., & Prout, A. (1998). *Theorizing childhood.* New York: Teachers College Press.

James, A., & Prout, A. (1997). *Constructing and reconstructing childhood: Contemporary issues in the sociological study of childhood.* London; Washington, DC: Falmer Press.

Jeffrey, B., & Troman, G. (2004). Time for ethnography. *British Educational Research Journal, 30*(4), 535–548.

Jenks, C. (Ed.) (2005). *Childhood* (vol. 2). New York: Psychology Press.

Jenks, C. (2008). Constructing childhood sociologically. In M, Kehily (Ed.), *Introduction to childhood studies* (pp. 93–111). Maidenhead, UK: Open University Press.

Juang, L. P., Qin, D. B., & Park, I. K. (2013). Deconstructing the myth of the "tiger mother": An introduction to the special issue on tiger parenting, Asian-heritage families, and child/adolescent well-being. *Asian American Journal of Psychology, 4*(1), 1–6.

Jupp, M. (1990). The UN convention on the rights of the child: An opportunity for advocates. *Human Rights Quaterly, 12*(1), 130–136.

Juzwik, M. (2004). Towards an ethics of answerability: Reconsidering dialogism in sociocultural literacy research. *College Composition and Communication, 55*(3), 536–567.

Kellet, M. (2006). "Just teach us the skills please, we'll do the rest": Empowering ten-year-olds as active researchers. *Children and Society, 18*, 329–343.

Kellogg, R. (1969). *Analyzing children's art.* Palo Alto, CA: Mayfield Publishing.

Kincheloe, J. L. (2005). Foreword. In L. Soto Diaz & B. B. Swadener (Eds), *Power and voice in research with children* (pp. xi–xii). New York, NY: Peter Lang.

Kindler, A. M., & Darras, B. (1997). Map of artistic development. In A. M. Kindler (Ed.), *Child development in art* (pp. 17–44). Reston, VA: National Art Education Association.

King, M. (2007). The right decision for the child. *The Modern Law Review, 70*, 857–871. https://doi.org/10.1111/j.1468-2230.2007.00667.x.

Kleinfeld, M. (2001). Childhood and child life: disClosure interviews with Jo Boyden, April 1, 2000. *disClosure: A Journal of Social Theory, 10*, 103–120.

Knight, L. M. (2018). Digital aesthetics and multidimensional play in early childhood. In C. Schulte, & C. Thompson (Eds), *Communities of practice: Art, play and aesthetics in early childhood* (pp. 133–152). Cham, Switzerland: Springer.

Knupfer, A. (1996). Ethnographic studies of children: The difficulties of entry, rapport, and presentations of their worlds. *International Journal of Qualitative Studies in Education, 9*(2), 135–149.

Kondo, K., & Sjöberg, U. (2012). Children's perspectives through the camera lens: Reflections on meaning-making processes and participatory research. *NORDICOM Review: Nordic Research on Media and Communication, 33*(1), 3.

Kouvou, O. (2016). Drawing with children: An experiment in assisted creativity. *International Journal of Art & Design Education, 35*(2), 275–290.

Kraftl, P. (2020). *after childhood: Re-thinking environment, materiality and media in children's lives* (1st ed.). Abingdon, OX, England and New York, NY: Routledge. https://doi.org/10.4324/9781315110011.

Kromidas, M. (2014). The 'savage' child and the nature of race: Posthuman interventions from New York City. *Anthropological Theory, 14*(4), 422–441. https://doi.org/10.1177/1463499614552739.

Kukkonen, T., & Chang-Kredl, S. (2018). Drawing as social play: Shared meaning-making in young children's collective drawing activities. *International Journal of Art & Design Education, 37*(1), 74–87.

Lampert, M. (2017). Beyond the politics of reception: Jacques Rancière and the politics of art. *Continental Philosophy Review, 50*(2), 181–200.

Lark-Horovitz, B., Lewis, H., & Luca, M. (1967). *Understanding children's art for better teaching* (1st ed.). Columbus, OH: Charles E. Merrill.

Latorre-Román, P. Á., Mora-López, D., & García-Pinillos, F. (2016). Intellectual maturity and physical fitness in preschool children. *Pediatrics International, 58*, 450–455. doi: 10.1111/ped.12898.

Leeds, J. A. (1989). The history of attitudes toward child art. *Studies in Art Education, 30*(2), 93–103.

LeVine, R. A. (2007). Ethnographic studies of childhood: A historical overview. *American Anthropologist, 109*(2), 247–260.

LeVine, R. A., & New, R. S. (2008). Introduction. In R. A. LeVine, & R. S. New (Eds), *Anthropology and child development: A cross-cultural reader* (pp. 1–11). Malden, MA: Blackwell.

Lewis, T. E. (2012). *The aesthetics of education: Theatre, curiosity, and politics in the work of Jacques Rancière and Paulo Freire.* New York, NY: Continuum International Pub. Group.

Lewis, T. E. (2015). "Move around! there is something to see here": The biopolitics of the perceptual pedagogy of the arts. *Studies in Art Education, 57*(1), 53–62.

Lewis, T. E. (2016a). The delicate taste for democracy: Rethinking the radical political possibilities of taste in visual culture art education. *Knowledge Cultures, 4*(5), 81–94.

Lewis, T. E. (2016b). Image as ignorant schoolmaster: A lesson in democratic equality. In D. Elliott, M. Silverman, & W. Bowman (Eds), *Artistic citizenship: Artistry, social responsibility, and ethical praxis* (pp. 549–562). Oxford University Press.

Lowenfeld, V., & Brittain, L. (1947). *Creative and mental growth: A textbook on art education.* New York: Macmillan.

Lowenfeld, V., & Michael, J. A. (1982). *The Lowenfeld lectures: Viktor Lowenfeld on art education and therapy.* University Park, PA: The Pennsylvania State University Press.

Maanen, J. V. (2011). *Tales of the field: On writing ethnography.* (2nd ed.). Chicago, IL: University of Chicago Press.

MacDonald, D. (1957). A theory of mass culture. In B. Rosenburg, & D. M. White (Eds), *Mass culture: The popular arts in America* (pp. 59–73). Glencoe, IL: Free Press.

MacNaughton, G. (2005). *Doing foucault in early childhood studies: Applying poststructural ideas.* London; New York: Routledge.

Maddern, J. F., & Adey, P. (2008). Editorial: Spectro-geographies. *Cultural Geographies, 15*(3), 291–295.

Malinowski, B. (1929). *The sexual life of savages: An ethnographic account of courtship, marriage, and family life among the Trobriand Islands, British New Guinea*. New York: Eugenics Publishing Company.

Mandell, N. (1988). The least-adult role in studying children. *Journal of Contemporary Ethnography*, *16*(4), 433–467.

Marshall, T. H. (1950). *Citizenship and social class*. Cambridge: Cambridge University Press.

Massumi, B. (2002). *Parables for the virtual: Movement, affect, sensation*. Durham, NC: Duke University Press.

Massumi, B. (2013). *Semblance and event: Activist philosophy and the occurrent arts* (First MIT Press paperback ed.). Cambridge, MA: MIT Press.

Matthews, H., & Limb, M. (1998). The right to say: The development of youth councils/forums within the UK. *Area (London 1969)*, *30*(1), 66–78. https://doi.org/10.1111/j.1475-4762.1998.tb00049.x.

Matthews, G. B. (2008). Getting beyond the deficit conception of childhood: Thinking philosophically with children. In M. Hand, & C. Winstanley (Eds), *Philosophy in schools* (pp. 27–40). London; New York: Continuum.

Matthews, G. B. (2009). Philosophy and developmental psychology: Outgrowing the deficit conception of childhood. In H. Siegel (Ed.), *The Oxford handbook of philosophy of education* (pp. 162–176). Oxford: Oxford University Press.

Matthews, J. (2003). *Drawing and painting: Children and visual representation* (2nd ed.). London: SAGE Publications Ltd.

May, T. (2008). *Political thought of Jacques Rancière: Creating equality*. Edinburgh: Edinburgh University Press.

May, T. (2010). Review of Jacques Rancière, Dissensus: On Politics and Aesthetics. *Notre Dame Philosophical Reviews*. Retrieved from https://ndpr.nd.edu/news/dissensus-on-politics-and-aesthetics/.

McClure, M. (2006). Thank heaven for little girls: Girls' drawings as representations of self. *Visual Culture and Gender*, *1*, 63–78.

McClure, M. (2007). Play as process: Choice, translation, reconfiguration, and the process of culture. *Visual Arts Research*, *33*(65), 63–70.

McClure, M. (2011). Child as totem: Redressing the myth of inherent creativity in early childhood. *Studies in Art Education*, *52*(2), 127–141. DOI: 10.1080/00393541.2011.11518829.

McClure, M. (2013). The monster and Lover♥Girl: Mapping complex relations in preschool children's digital video productions. *Studies in Art Education*, *55*(1), 18–34.

Mead, M. (1928). *Coming of age in Samoa*. New York: William Morrow.

Michael, J. A., & Morris, J. W. (1985). Influences of the theory and philosophy of Victor Lowenfeld. *Studies in Art Education, 26*(2), 103–110.

Mills, C. W. (1959). *The sociological imagination*. New York: Oxford University Press.

Mitchell, C. & Reid-Walsh, J. (2002). *Researching children's Popular culture: The cultural Spaces of childhood*. London; New York: Taylor & Francis Group.

Moosa-Mitha, M. (2005). A difference-centred alternative to theorization of children's citizenship rights. *Citizenship Studies, 9*(4), 369–388.

Oakley, A. (1994). Women and children first and last: Parallels and differences between children's and women's studies. In B. Myall (Ed.), *Children's childhood observed and experienced* (pp. 13–32). London: Falmer Press.

Park, H. (2018). Creative collaborations: Emergent play in the preschool art studio. *Art Education, 71*(5), 14–19.

Park, H. (2019). Drawing together: Towards a relational ethics of ignorance. In C. M. Schulte (Ed.), *Ethics and research with young children: "New" perspectives* (pp. 37–48). London: Bloomsbury.

Park, H. (2021). Bad hands and big black dots: Dissensual politics in the kindergarten classroom. *Studies in Art Education, 62*(1), 10–22. https://doi.org/10.1080/003935 41.2020.1858262.

Park, H., & Schulte, C. M. (2021). *Visual arts with young children: Practices, pedagogies, and learning*. New York, NY: Routledge.

Park, S., Lim, H., & Choi, H. (2015). "Gangnam mom": A qualitative study on the information behaviors of Korean helicopter mothers. In *iConference 2015 Proceedings*. Retrieved from https://www.ideals.illinois.edu/handle/2142/73636.

Pearson, P. (2001). Towards a theory of children's drawing as social practice. *Studies in Art Education, 42*(4), 348–365.

Pérez de Miles, A. (2016). The antinomy of autonomy and heteronomy in contemporary art practice. *Knowledge Cultures, 4*(5), 43–60.

Piaget, J. (1932). *The moral judgement of the child*. New York: Collier.

Piaget, J. (1960). *The psychology of intelligence*. Paterson, NJ: Littlefield.

Piaget, J. (1962). *Play, dreams, and imitation in childhood* (vol. N171). New York: Norton.

Piaget, J. (1971). *Structuralism*. New York: Harper & Row.

Piaget, J., & Inhelder, B. (1956). *The child's conception of space*. London: Routledge and Kegan Paul.

Piaget, J. & Inhelder, B. (1969). Intellectual operations and their development. In P. Fraise & J. Piaget (Eds), *Experimental psychology: Its scope and method* (vol. 7) (pp. 144–205). London: Routledge & Kegan Paul.

Pacini-Ketchabaw, V., Kind, S., & Kocher, L. L. (2016). *Encounters with materials in early childhood education*. New York: Routledge.

Picard, D. (2015). Sex differences in scores on the draw-a-person test across childhood: Do they relate to graphic fluency? *Perceptual and Motor Skills, 120*(1), 273–287.

Pierce, C. & Allen, G. (1975). Childism. *Psychiatric Annals, 5*(7), 15–24.

Plato, & Burnet, J. (1902). *Platonis opera*. New York; Oxonii: E Typographeo Clarendoniano.

Prout, A. (2011). Taking a step away from modernity: Reconsidering the new sociology of childhood. *Global Studies of Childhood, 1*(1), 4–14.

Qvortrup, J. (1993). Societal position of childhood: The international project childhood as a social phenomenon. *Childhood, 1*(2), 119–124.

Qvortrup, J. (2000). Macroanalysis of childhood. In P. Christensen, & A. James (Eds), *Research with children* (pp. 77–98). London: Falmer.

Qvortrup, J., Bardy, M., Sgritta, G., & Wintersberger, H. (1994). *Childhood matters: Social theory, practice and politics*. Aldershot: Avebury Press.

Rancière, J. ([1974] 2011). *Althusser's lesson*. (E. Battista, Trans.). London; New York: Continuum.

Rancière, J. (1989). *The nights of labor: The workers' dream in nineteenth-century France*. Philadelphia, PA: Temple University Press.

Rancière, J. (1991). *The ignorant schoolmaster: Five lessons in intellectual emancipation* (1st ed.) (K. Ross, Trans.). Stanford, CA: Stanford University Press.

Rancière, J. (1992). Politics, identification, and subjectivization. *October, 61*(61), 58–64.

Rancière, J. (1995). *On the shores of politics*. (L. Heron, Trans.). London: Verso.

Rancière, J. (1999). *Dis-agreement: Politics and philosophy*. Minneapolis: University of Minnesota Press.

Rancière, J. (2001). Ten theses on politics. *Theory and Event, 5*(3).

Rancière, J. (2002). The aesthetic revolution and its outcomes. *New Left Review, 14*, 133–51.

Rancière, J. (2003). *The philosopher and his poor*. London; Durham, NC: Duke University Press.

Rancière, J. (2004a). *The flesh of words: The politics of writing*. Stanford, CA: Stanford University Press.

Rancière, J. (2004b). *Aesthetics and its discontents*. Cambridge; Malden, MA: Polity Press.

Rancière, J. (2006a). Our police order: What can be said, seen, and done. *Le Monde Diplomatique* (Oslo), November 8, 2006.

Rancière, J. (2006b). Thinking between disciplines: An aesthetics of knowledge. *Parrhesia*, *1*, 1–12.

Rancière, J. (2006c). *Hatred of democracy* (Steve Corcoran, Trans.). London: Verso.

Rancière, J. (2009a). The emancipated spectator. *Artforum XLV*, (7) (March), 271–280.

Rancière, J. (2009b). *The aesthetic unconscious* (English ed.). Cambridge, UK: Polity.

Rancière, J. (2009c). Contemporary art and the politics of aesthetics. In B. Hinderliter, V. Maimon, J. Mansoor, & S. McCormick (Eds), *Communities of sense: Rethinking aesthetics and politics* (pp. 31–50). Durham, NC: Duke University Press.

Rancière, J. (2009d). *The future of the image*. London; New York: Verso.

Rancière, J. (2010). On ignorant schoolmasters. In C. Bingham, & G. Biesta (Eds), *Jacques Rancière: Education, truth, emancipation* (pp. 1–24). London; New York: Bloomsbury Academic.

Rancière, J. (2011). *The emancipated spectator* (Reprint edition). London: Verso.

Rancière, J. (2013a). *The politics of aesthetics: The distribution of the sensible*. London; New York: Bloomsbury Academic.

Rancière, J. (2013b). *Aisthesis: Scenes from the aesthetic regime of art*. (Z. Paul, Trans.) (1st ed.). London; New York: Verso.

Rancière, J. (2015). *Dissensus: On politics and aesthetics*. (S. Corcoran, Trans.) (Reprint edition). London; New York: Bloomsbury Academic.

Rancière, J. (2016). *The method of equality: Interviews with Laurent Jeanpierre and Dork Zabunyan* (J. Rose, Trans.). Cambridge: Polity.

Rancière, J. (2017). *Dissenting words: Interviews with Jacques Rancière* (E. Battista, Ed. & Trans.). London; New York: Bloomsbury Publishing.

Reinach, A. (1913/1983). The apriori foundations of civil law. *Aletheia: An International Journal of Philosophy*, *3*, 1–142.

Richardson (Eisenhauer), J. (2018). The art and politics of artists with mental disabilities experiencing confinement. *Studies in Art Education*, *59*(1), 8–21.

Richardson, J., & (Eisenhauer) Richardson, J. (2020). Bill Shannon: Challenging disabling environments and redistributing sense. In J. Derby, & A. Wexler (Eds), *Contemporary art and culture in disability studies* (pp. 146–156). New York: Routledge.

Richardson, L., & St. Pierre, E. A. (2005). Writing: A method of inquiry. In N. K. Denzin, & Y. S. Lincoln (Eds), *The SAGE handbook of qualitative research* (pp. 959–978). Thousand Oaks, CA: Sage Publications Ltd.

Rinaldi, C. (1998). The spaces of childhood. In G. Ceppi, & M. Zini (Eds), *Children, spaces relations: Metaproject for an environment for young children* (pp. 114–120). Reggio Emilia, Italy: Reggio Children.

Rockhill, G. (2013). Editor's introduction. In J. Rancière (Ed.), *The politics of aesthetics: The distribution of the sensible* (pp. xi–xvii). London: Bloomsbury.

Rollo, T. (2018). The color of childhood: The role of the child/human binary in the production of anti-Black racism. *Journal of Black Studies, 49*(4), 307–329. https://doi.org/10.1177/0021934718760769.

Rosen, M. (2018). The data have landed. February 8, 2018. Available at: http://michaelrosenblog.blogspot.com/2018/02/the-data-have-landed.html (accessed February 3, 2019).

Rosen, R. (2017). Between play and the quotidian: Inscriptions of monstrous characters on the racialised bodies of children. *Race Ethnicity and Education, 20*(2), 178–191.

Ross, K. (1991). Translator's introduction. In J. Rancière, *The ignorant schoolmaster: Five lessons in intellectual emancipation* (pp. vii–xxiii). (K. Ross, Trans.). Stanford, CA: Stanford University Press.

Sakr, M. (2017). "We're just gonna scribble it": The affective and social work of destruction in children's art-making with different semiotic resources. *Contemporary Issues in Early Childhood, 18*(2), 227–239.

Sakr, M. (2019). Children's photography as sense-making. In M. Sakr, & J. Osgood (Eds), *Postdevelopmental approaches to childhood art* (pp. 47–66). London: Bloomsbury.

Sakr, M. & Osgood, J. (2019). *Postdevelopmental approaches to childhood art*. London: Bloomsbury Academic.

Schulte, C. M. (2011). Verbalization in children's drawing performances: Toward a metaphorical continuum of inscription, extension, and re-inscription. *Studies in Art Education, 53*(1), 20–34.

Schulte, C. M. (2015a). Lines of deterritorialization: The becoming-minor of Carter's drawing. *Studies in Art Education, 56*(2), 142–155. DOI:10.1080/00393541.2015.11518957

Schulte, C. M. (2015b). Intergalactic encounters: Desire and the political immediacy of children's drawing. *Studies in Art Education, 56*(3), 241–256. DOI:10.1080/00393541.2015.11518966

Schulte, C. M. (2018). The will-to-research children's drawing. In C. M. Schulte, & C. M. Thompson (Eds), *Communities of practice: Art, play, and aesthetics in early childhood* (pp. 213–228). New York: Springer International Publishing.

Schulte, C. M. (2021). Childhood drawing: The making of a deficit aesthetic. *Global Studies of Childhood, 11*(1), 54–68. https://doi.org/10.1177/2043610621995821.

Schulte, C. M., & Thompson, C. M. (Eds). (2018). *Communities of practice: Art, play, and aesthetics in early childhood*. Cham, Switzerland: Springer International.

Sedley, D. (2016). An introduction to Plato's theory of forms. *Royal Institute of Philosophy Supplement, 78*, 3–22. DOI:10.1017/S1358246116000333

Shayan, T. (2022). The culture of childhood in (and) spaces of resistance. *Contemporary Issues in Early Childhood, 23*(2), 122–138. https://doi.org/10.1177/1463949120966105.

Shin, R. (2016). "Gangnam Style" and global visual culture. *Studies in Art Education, 57*(3), 252–264.

Shin, R., & Kim, J. (2014). A comparative cross-cultural examination of community art education programs in South Korea and the United States. *Studies in Art Education, 55*(3), 227–240.

Skarpenes, O., & Sæverot, A. M. (2018). Symmetry and equality: Bringing Rancière into the classroom. *Contemporary Issues in Early Childhood, 19*(1), 63–71.

Smith, L. T. (2012). *Decolonizing methodologies: Research and indigenous peoples* (2nd ed.). London: Zed Books.

Springgay, S., & Zaliwska, Z. (2015). Diagrams and cuts: A materialist approach to research-creation. *Cultural Studies ↔ Critical Methodologies, 15*(2), 136–144. https://doi.org/10.1177/1532708614562881.

Stake, R. E. (2005). Qualitative case studies. In N. K. Denzin, & Y. S. Lincoln (Eds), *The Sage handbook of qualitative research* (3rd ed.). (pp. 443–466). Thousand Oaks, CA: Sage Publications.

Stocking, G. (1987). *Victorian anthropology*. New York: The Free Press.

Subject. (n.d.). In *Oxford English Dictionaries Online*. Retrieved from https://en.oxforddictionaries.com/definition/subject.

Sully, J. (1896). *Studies of childhood*. New York: D. Appleton Company.

Sully, J. (1907). *Children's ways: Being selections from the author's "Studies of Childhood,": With some additional matter.* New York, NY: D. Appleton.

Sunday, K. E. (2015). Relational making: Re/imagining theories of child art. *Studies in Art Education, 56*(3), 228–240.

Sunday, K. E. (2018). Drawing and storytelling as political action: Difference, plurality and coming into presence in the early childhood classroom. *International Journal of Art & Design Education, 37*(1), 6–17.

Tanke, J. J. (2011). *Jacques Rancière: An introduction*. London: A&C Black.

Tarr, P. (2003). Reflections on the image of the child: Reproducer or creator of culture. *Art Education, 56*(4), 6–11.

Tavin, K. (2005). Hauntological shifts: Fear and loathing of popular (visual) culture, *Studies in Art Education, 46*(2), 101–117.

Tavin, K. & Hausman, J. (2004). Art education and visual culture in the age of globalization. *Art Education (Reston), 57*(5), 47–53. https://doi.org/10.1080/00043125.2004.11653568.

Templeton, T. (2021). Whose story is it? Thinking through early childhood with young children's photographs. *Occasional Paper Series, 2021 (45)*. Retrieved from https://educate.bankstreet.edu/occasional-paper-series/vol2021/iss45/8.

Thompson, C. M. (1995). "What should I draw today?": Sketchbooks in early childhood. *Art Education, 48*(5), 6–11.

Thompson, C. M. (2002). Drawing together: Peer influence in preschool-kindergarten art classes. In L. Bresler, & C. M. Thompson (Eds), *The arts in children's lives: Context, culture, and curriculum* (pp. 129–138). Boston, MA: Kluwer Academic Press.

Thompson, C. M. (2003). Kinderculture in the art classroom: Early childhood art and the mediation of culture. *Studies in Art Education, 44*(2), 135–146.

Thompson, C. M. (2006). The ket aesthetic: Visual culture in childhood. In J. Fineberg (Ed.), *When we were young: New perspectives on the art of the child* (pp. 31–43). Berkeley: University of California Press.

Thompson, C. M. (2009). Mira! Looking, listening, and lingering in research with children. *Visual Arts Research, 35*(1), 24–34.

Thompson, C. M. (2017). Listening for stories: Childhood studies and art education. *Studies in Art Education, 58*(1), 7–16.

Thompson, C. M., & Bales, S. (1991). "Michael doesn't like my dinosaurs": Conversations in a preschool art class. *Studies in Art Education, 33*(1), 43–55.

Thorne, B. (1993). *Gender play: Girls and boys in school*. New Brunswick, NJ: Rutgers University Press.

Thumlert, K. (2015). Affordances of equality: Rancière, emerging media, and the new amateur. *Studies in Art Education, 56*(2), 114–126.

Trafí-Prats, L. (2012). Urban children and intellectual emancipation: Video narratives of self and place in the city of Milwaukee. *Studies in Art Education, 53*(2), 125–138.

UN General Assembly (1989). Convention on the rights of the child. *Treaty series, 1577*, 3, United Nations. Available at: http://www.refworld.org/docid/3ae6b38f0.html.

van Gennep, A. (1960). *The rites of passage* (M. B. Vizedom, & G. L. Caffee, Trans.). Chicago, IL: University of Chicago Press.

Vannini, P. (2015). *Non-representational methodologies: Re-envisioning research*. London; New York: Routledge, Taylor & Francis Group.

Vellanki, V., & Davesar, U. (2020). (Re)imagining visual research beyond photovoice: Methodological explorations with a young photographer. *Review of Education, Pedagogy, and Cultural Studies, 42*(3), 217–239.

Viola, W. (1936). *Child art and Franz Cizek*. Vienna: Austrian Junior Red Cross.

Vlieghe, J. (2018). Rethinking emancipation with Freire and Rancière: A plea for a thing-centred pedagogy. *Educational Philosophy and Theory, 50*(10), 917–927. DOI: 10.1080/00131857.2016.1200002

Walsh, D. J. (2005). Developmental theory and early childhood education: Necessary but not sufficient. In N. Yelland (Ed.), *Critical issues in early childhood education* (pp. 40–48). England: Open University.

Ware, R. (1973). Acts and action. *The Journal of Philosophy, 70*(13), 403–418.

Weisner, T. S., & Gallimore, R. (1977). My brother's keeper: Child and sibling caretaking. *Current Anthropology, 18*(2), 169–190.

Williams, R. (1976). *Keywords: A vocabulary of culture and society*. London: Fontana.

Wilson, B. (1974). The superheroes of J. C. Holtz plus an outline of a theory of child art. *Art Education, 16*(1), 2–9.

Wilson, B. (1997). Child art, multiple interpretations, and conflicts of interest. In A. M. Kindler (Ed.), *Child development in art* (pp. 81–94). Reston, VA: The National Art Education Association.

Wilson, B. (2003). Three sites for visual cultural pedagogy: Honoring students' interests and imagery. *International Journal of Arts Education, 1*(3), 107–126.

Wilson, B. (2004). Child art after modernism: Visual culture and new narratives. In E. Eisner, & M. Day (Eds), *Handbook for research and policy in art education* (pp. 299–328). Mahwah, NJ: Erlbaum.

Wilson, B. (2005). More lessons from the superheroes of J. C. Holz: The visual culture of childhood and the third pedagogical site. *Art Education, 58*(6), 18–34.

Wilson, B. (2007). Art, visual culture, and child/adult collaborative images: Recognizing the other-than. *Visual Arts Research, 33*(2), 6–20.

Wilson, B. (2008a). Contemporary art, the best of art, and third-site pedagogy. *Art Education, 61*(2), 6–9.

Wilson, B. (2008b). Research at the margins of schooling: Biographical inquiry and third-site pedagogy. *International Journal of Education through Art, 4*(2), 119–130.

Wilson, B., & Wilson, M. (1981). The use and uselessness of developmental stages. *Art Education, 34*(5), 4.

Wilson, B., & Wilson, M. (1984). A tale of four cultures: The story drawings of American, Australian, Egyptian and Finnish children. In R. Ott, & A. Hurwitz (Eds), *Art and education: International perspectives* (pp. 31–38). University Park: The Pennsylvania State University Press.

Wilson, M. & Wilson, B. (1982). *Teaching children to draw*. Englewood Cliffs: PrenticeHall.

Wolcott, H. F. (1999). *Ethnography: A way of seeing*. Walnut Creek, CA: AltaMira Press.

Yin, R. K. (2014). *Case study research: Design and methods* (5th ed.). Thousand Oaks, CA: Sage Publications.

Yoon, H. S. (2018). "The imperial march" toward early literacy: Locating popular culture in a kindergarten classroom. *Language Arts, 95*(3), 171–181.

Zurn, P. (2021). *Curiosity and power: The politics of inquiry*. Minneapolis: University of Minnesota Press.

Index